SAINT
FRANCIS
of ASSISI
A LIFE INSPIRED

About Wyatt North Publishing

Starting out with just one writer, Wyatt North Publishing has expanded to include writers from across the country. Our writers include college professors, religious theologians, and historians.

Wyatt North Publishing provides high quality, perfectly formatted, original books.

Send us an email and we will personally respond within 24 hours! As a boutique publishing company we put our readers first and never respond with canned or automated emails. Send us an email at hello@WyattNorth.com, and you can visit us at www.WyattNorth.com.

Introduction

While St. Francis of Assisi is one of the most beloved saints in history, the relevancy of St. Francis for our times in light of the election of Pope Francis has yet to be explored. This book is written with the intention of filling that gap. While it is biographical in nature, it also freely explores themes that relate to St. Francis but are not a part of his life. This book is about more than the life of St. Francis of Assisi; it is about the impact this beloved saint has had through his imitation of Christ, his love of poverty, the Franciscan movement, and his profound influence on Pope Francis.

This book explores classic spiritual themes across the centuries, from medieval Europe to the modern world. In some parts of the book, the geopolitical landscapes are vastly different from our world today, but the problems facing humanity are extremely similar because of our fallen human nature, which is always in need of reform. Here is where the genius of St. Francis comes into play. The enduringness of the spirituality of Francis is no accident but, rather, is based on the attractiveness of Christ as portrayed in the Gospels. St. Francis's call is essentially a call to return to the basics of Christianity. It is a call to Christians to reach back to their roots so that their spiritual lives can draw strength from the pure waters of the Gospel instead of being choked by manmade traditions and worldly concerns. In the words of G. K. Chesterton, the coming of Francis "marked the moment when men could be reconciled not only to God but to nature and, most difficult of all, to themselves. ... his whole function [was] to tell men to start afresh and, in that sense, to tell them to forget" (124).

This same theme can be found in the message of Pope Francis today. He insists that only by returning to the Gospel are Christians able to be faithful to the call of Jesus. Pope Francis recognizes the profoundness of St. Francis's message and has signaled his intent to align his papacy with the message of the *poverello* from Assisi. In an age when the poor are getting poorer and the rich are getting richer, and in which globalization has the potential to bind human beings more closely together, the call of St. Francis is more relevant than ever. Christians in the world must not turn a blind eye to the suffering of so many millions of people today, many of whom are dying of starvation. As Jesus indicated, we must attend to the needs of the poorest if we hope to be shown mercy on the Day of Judgment.

Another theme that will be addressed is the relationship between St. Francis and nature. St. Francis was an ardent lover of creation and took literally the evangelical injunction to preach the Gospel to all creation (Mk 16:15) to the extent that he even instructed the birds to praise their creator. Francis's life was in harmony with God, with his fellow human beings, and with the rest of God's creatures. With the disregard for the natural environment that many people have today, the call to seek harmony with creation is of the utmost importance. This is why St. Francis of Assisi was declared the patron saint of the environment.

Finally, this book investigates the theme of holiness and a deepening spirituality. What made Francis so holy? How might we begin to follow in St. Francis's footsteps so as to become closer to God? St. Francis, inflamed with love by the seraphim, the flaming angel of God, serves as a model for all to follow, not only religious. His call is the call to simplicity and to evangelical perfection, but this is simply the call of Jesus that is addressed to everyone. After all, Jesus instructed his disciples to be perfect as God the Father is perfect (Mt 5:48). For this reason, we have to open our ears to what the spirit of God is saying to the churches and to us (Rv 2:29). By imitating St. Francis, who imitated Jesus, who is the image of the invisible God (Col 1:15), we are able to draw closer to the Father and to become icons of the Father to all who come in contact with us. This kind of spiritual imitation is scriptural since St. Paul asked the Corinthians to imitate him as he imitates Christ (1 Cor 11:1). By way of this mimesis, therefore, we are able to become imitators of God and to spread his goodness to all of creation. Of all the imitators of Christ, St. Francis offered perhaps the most famous approach, which features poverty, simplicity, and flaming charity. May this account of the legacy of St. Francis inspire many to follow Christ more closely.

Come Holy Spirit, enter the hearts of your faithful, and enkindle in them the fire of your love.

Send forth your spirit, and they shall be created, and you shall renew the face of the earth!
Amen.

Beginnings

In 1181 or 1182 was born one of the most beloved Catholic saints of all time, St. Francis of Assisi. He was born Giovanni di Pietro di Bernardone to Pietro di Bernardone and Pica de Bourlemont. Pietro was an Italian merchant, and Pica was a French noblewoman. Although Pica baptized him Giovanni (John) while Pietro was away on a business trip, when Pietro came back, he became accustomed to calling him Francesco ("the Frenchman"), and the nickname stuck.

Assisi was a small city during the time of St. Francis, with a population of no more than two or three thousand. His family was counted as being in the top-third tax bracket of Assisi, and Thomas of Celano, one of St. Francis's earliest biographers, describes him as coming from an exceptionally wealthy family.

Although Francis was not learned, he was intelligent. He picked up French, most likely during business trips with his father. In fact, he knew French well enough to hold a conversation, sing songs, and write poetry, which he loved. He was also familiar with Latin. Francis acquired knowledge of accounting through his apprenticeship in his father's business when he was about fourteen years old.

St. Bonaventure, the Franciscan professor at the University of Paris who was a contemporary of St. Thomas Aquinas, describes the coming of St. Francis in dramatic words:

> *In these last days the grace of God our Savior has appeared* in his servant Francis. ... He *preached* to men *the Gospel of peace* and salvation, being himself *the Angel* of true *peace*. Like John the Baptist he was appointed by God *to prepare in the desert a way* of the highest poverty ... he was also assigned an angelic ministry and was totally aflame with a Seraphic fire. Like a hierarchic man he was lifted up in *a fiery chariot* ... he came *in the spirit and power of Elijah*. (Bonaventure, 179-181)

This passage clearly manifests the esteem St. Bonaventure had for his spiritual father, St. Francis.

Yet, Bonaventure makes clear that, initially, Francis had not been yet been captured by Christ. Bonaventure remarks that when Francis was a young man, he "was distracted by the external affairs of his father's business and drawn down toward earthly things by the corruption of human nature"

(Bonaventure, *The Soul's Journey Into God; The Tree of Life; The Life of St. Francis*, 187). Francis was the leader of a group of boys from wealthy families, and his generosity gave him the reputation of being prodigal. During this time, he also exhibited an intense aversion to lepers, which he later overcame.

When he was twenty-two years old, Francis joined a militia as a result of a dispute between Perugia and Assisi. Since he was able to afford a horse, Francis avoided service as a foot soldier. Assisi and its allies fought against Perugia, but unfortunately for Francis, he and his friends were captured and put in prison for about a year. He was released in 1203, but life in prison took a toll on his health. Moreover, he had experienced war and had seen his friends killed in battle.

Despite this episode, Francis signed up for a new military expedition in 1205. He had a dream about spoils piled high, and when he asked for whom these riches were intended, he heard the reply that they were for him and his men. Taking the dream literally, Francis thought that it meant he would be victorious in battle. Later on, however, he dreamt that he heard a voice asking him whether it was better to serve the master or the servant. When he replied that it was better to serve the master, he was asked, "Then why do you serve the servant?" Disturbed, he confided in a friend, telling him that he was no longer interested in the military because of that dream.

Francis was twelve miles away from Assisi at that time. He sold his goods, including his horse, and walked back to Assisi. When he was two miles away from Assisi, he spent the night at the church of San Damiano, originally a Benedictine priory, which was in sore need of renovations.

The next day, Francis returned to Assisi. There he found no joy in the life he had lived before. His friends noticed that he was a different man than the jovial youth who had funded their lavish parties. Rather than enlivening his friends, he was somber and pensive. Francis ceased attending such parties and stopped working at his father's business. Francis had been changed by his experience of war.

Not finding peace, Francis made a pilgrimage to Rome and prayed at St. Peter's tomb. He threw a large sum of money at the tomb and traded clothes with a beggar, after which he began to ask for alms. He wanted not only to give alms, but wanted to see what being poor was like. What did it mean to walk around, depending on the charity of others? What kind of life would this be like? This was an important step in what was to culminate in Francis's pure embrace of Lady Poverty. After making his way back to Rome, he began to stay and pray frequently at the church of San Damiano, to which he eventually became attached as a penitent. Before this occurred, however, Francis began caring for lepers, whom he had previously feared.

Leprosy, a horrific disease that literally eats away at people's flesh, often leaves lepers horribly disfigured. Francis, however, filled with the strength of God, ministered to the lepers, finding in them the presence of Christ. By serving the lepers, Francis realized that he was serving Jesus himself. On top of this, he was moved with genuine compassion and love toward these individuals, whose disease, though causing their flesh to rot, could not diminish their inherent human dignity. They too deserved to be loved and cared for despite their hideous appearance. He decided to live with the lepers and to care for their physical and spiritual needs by dressing their wounds, bathing them, and treating them with respect.

What can we say of this beginning in relation to Pope Francis? Pope Francis is ethnically Italian, as was St. Francis. Jorge

Bergoglio was born in 1936 in Buenos Aires to Italian immigrants. Furthermore, both suffered extreme sickness in youth. When Bergoglio was twenty-one, he had a serious case of pneumonia and a part of his lung had to be removed. Both men came from fairly large families, at least by today's standards: Bergoglio was the oldest out of five children, and Francis was one of seven. It seems that the illnesses, trials, communities, and orientations to poverty of the two men affected their spirituality, albeit in different ways, and helped to shape their later lives and characters.

Francis Renounces the World

Francis was drawn to the humble church of San Damiano that he had visited on his way back from his second short-lived military expedition. There, in the midst of fervent prayer before the crucifix, Francis heard a voice tell him to repair God's house. Francis joyfully consented, thinking that renovating the church of San Damiano was his mission. He rushed back to Assisi, gathered money and supplies, and returned to San Damiano. The priest at San Damiano was skeptical that Francis was serious about restoring the church. Francis began rebuilding the church with his own hands, determined to fulfill his divine quest. He was savvy enough to realize that his father would be furious when he found out that Francis was using his money to repair a church, so he prepared a cellar or a crypt in which he could hide when his father eventually came to look for him.

After several weeks, however, Francis mustered enough courage to go back to Assisi. When he arrived in the city, he was greeted with scorn and ridicule since he looked like a madman. Upon hearing the commotion and discovering that Francis had come back, Pietro sent his men to apprehend his son and had him locked in the cellar of his house. It was only when Pietro left for his annual business trip to France that

Pica, Francis's mother, let Francis go. Francis went back to San Damiano.

From a business perspective, Pietro's actions seem to be somewhat warranted. After all, he was a wealthy merchant, and Francis was entitled to half of his mother's dowry. Although Francis's brother was an adept businessman, Pietro could not count on Francis, whom he feared would squander his portion of the inheritance on renovating the church at San Damiano. It was bad enough that Francis was frittering his inheritance away; now Francis was the butt of jokes among the townsfolk, thus rendering him a blemish on the family name. These developments were detrimental to the family's prestige in Assisi, which for Pietro was intolerable.

Upon returning and finding out that Pica had released Francis, Pietro summoned Francis to court. At first, Francis was summoned by the secular consuls. Being astute, Francis claimed that since he was an ecclesiastic, the secular law did not have jurisdiction over him. When the bishop summoned him, however, Francis willingly left San Damiano and went to meet his father and the bishop, who urged Francis to give his father his property and his money. Francis willingly gave up his right to the dowry, stripped himself of his fine clothes, and placed the money on top of the clothes, saying that he wanted to call God his father, rather than Pietro. The bishop then took Francis under his mantle, and Pietro went on his way.

Now Francis was entirely free of worldly cares. With God as his father and with no possessions, Francis set out to start a new life. Of course, it not entirely new; after all, he still had to finish rebuilding the church of San Damiano. How was he to renovate the church, though, without any money?

Francis had an ingenious solution. In what G. K. Chesterton describes as an inverted parable (42), instead of begging for bread, Francis begged for stones from passersby. With these stones, Francis began rebuilding the church of San Damiano. He labored drudgingly with the stones until he completed his project. Stone after stone, he repaired and reconfigured the church of San Damiano. Could Francis have realized at this time that his call was not, primarily, to rebuild a physical church but rather to build up the universal Church of God? This is exactly what Francis's vocation was—to build up the church of Christ, which had fallen into ruins. Francis's charge was to reinvigorate the Lord's people by calling them back to repentance, as if he were a second John the Baptist.

Once finished with his original project of renovating the church of San Damiano, Francis continued his architectural endeavors by repairing the church of St. Mary of the Angels at the Portiuncula. In addition to these two churches, Francis also repaired a church that was dedicated to St. Peter. The fact that Francis worked on rebuilding these three churches has been attributed all sorts of symbolisms by Francis's biographers. What can be said beyond the shadow of a doubt is that these rebuilding projects served two functions: the first, to fulfill literally the call of God to Francis to rebuild his church; and the second, to foreshadow Francis's rebuilding of the universal Church, which was also in need of repair.

What is the state of the universal church today? Is it in shambles? That would be an exaggeration; however, the Catholic Church is reeling from the sex abuse scandal that rocked the Church around the turn of the millennium. Sadly, the wicked deeds of a small percentage of priests and the subsequent cover-ups by several bishops have had a profoundly negative impact on the perception of the Catholic Church. Compounded with this, the ethics of the Church, especially in relation to sexuality, are accused by others of being antiquated and off the mark. In the Western world, where religion is more and more frequently the target of atheistic verbal attacks, the Catholic Church is often ridiculed and mocked. At the same time, there are signs of growth, especially in third-world nations of Africa and South America, and elsewhere in the Southern Hemisphere.

Is it a coincidence that Pope Francis is the first pope from the Southern Hemisphere? Demographically, it is no surprise, despite the fact that he is the first non-European pope since Pope Gregory III in 741. Pope Francis recognizes that, in many ways, the Catholic Church is experiencing multiple crises and is in need of a radical renewal. For this reason, he has called on Catholics to go back to the simplicity of the Gospel message and to follow Jesus. Christians must enkindle within them the flame of God's love and spread the Gospel throughout the world; and the only way they will be successful in this endeavor is to imitate Christ, which was St. Francis's sole goal in life. By dedicating themselves to serving Christ and imitating him, Christians will be able to serve the poor, thus being true disciples of Jesus Christ. In this age of globalization and capitalism, such Christianity is more necessary than ever.

Francis's First Followers

Francis's *modus vivendi* from around 1206 to 1209 was to repair his churches, to care for the lepers, to beg for his daily food, and to pray before the crucifix. He did not expect to start a movement or to live in a community with anyone. Francis was an itinerant—a sort of penitent freelancer, if you will. For this reason, he was surprised when two men met him, wanting to imitate his way of life.

The first man who intended to follow Francis was Bernard of Quintavalle, a wealthy young man. After speaking to Francis in 1208, he literally sold everything he had and gave his money to the poor. After this, he joined Francis and imitated his life of prayer and penance. At nearly the same time, a man named Peter joined them. He was an older man who was poorer than Bernard had been. These two men, in contrast to the other citizens of Assisi, decided to follow Francis even though he appeared to many to be out of his mind. They perceived the movement of the Holy Spirit within Francis, a humble man who would eventually catch the world on fire with the love of Jesus and the simplicity of the Gospel.

Now that Francis had brothers, he wanted to receive ecclesiastical approval for his way of life. There was one problem, however. Both Don Peter, the priest at San Damiano, and Bishop Guido were absent for some reason or another. In order to get advice on what he should do, Francis went into Assisi with his two brothers and approached the parish priest of the church of San Nicolò di Piazza. He asked the priest to perform a *sortes biblicae*, a practice in vogue at the time that consisted of opening up the Bible three times and receiving a commentary by a clergyman as to what God was telling an individual through the Scriptures. Francis thereby hoped to gain insight into God's will for him and his companions. In response, the priest opened up the missal to the following three passages: Mark 10:17-21, Luke 9:1-6, and Matthew 16:24-28. Taken together, these three scriptural passages portray a radical way of life and eventually formed the basis for the entire Franciscan rule. The three men carefully memorized these texts and kept them ever before their hearts.

After this encounter, Francis and his companions lived together for about a year. Francis still did not have approval for his way of life, although he had been given guidance as to what it should be. Since Don Peter and Guido were still away, he became determined to acquire approval by going to Rome. Francis and his companions therefore undertook a several-day journey to Rome. At the Lateran, they unexpectedly met Bishop Guido, who was upset that these men were seeking a way of life from the pope instead of going through him first. After explaining to Guido that their intentions were sincere and that they were only striving to do the will of God, Francis managed to acquire Guido's assistance.

Guido's contact in the papal court was Cardinal John of San Paulo Colonna. Cardinal Colonna most likely regarded Francis's motley crew as merely another of the many religious movements that were cropping up at this particular time in medieval Europe. The cardinal gave a hearing to Francis and his brothers but advised them to join another established group. Perhaps he thought their intention was to be hermits. In the end, the cardinal agreed to bring their case before the pope.

Cardinal Colonna presented his case to Pope Innocent III, most likely without Francis and his two companions in attendance. According to St. Bonaventure, Innocent had a dream that Francis was holding up the Lateran basilica and was keeping it from collapsing. This certainly would explain the quick acceptance of Francis's rule. After accepting their little rule, the pope gave the men his apostolic blessing and told them to preach penance and to increase in numbers, thus constituting the group as one of lay preachers. This was a surprising turn for the brothers. Francis had no aspirations to preaching, although he was passionate about penance. He and his companions were tonsured, a sign that they were officially men of the Church and had authority to preach.

Francis, however, was not known as a preacher. In fact, there is a saying attributed to him that Christians are always to preach the Gospel, but to use words only when necessary. This saying sums up rather well his attitude toward preaching: one's way of life, rather than words, was to be one's primary testimony of Christ.

Before the men left, Francis had a dream that a giant tree stood in front of him. As he approached, he began to grow to such an extent that he was able to bend down and place his hand on the tree. Recalling this dream to his brothers, Francis believed that it applied to them since the pope had listened to Francis's request. After visiting the tomb of the apostle Peter, they made their way back to Assisi, no doubt filled with joy but also harboring some uncertainty as to what their new way of life was actually calling them to do.

Francis's at having been received by the pope and at having his proposal approved so quickly must have been similar to the emotions Jorge Bergoglio experienced upon being elected to the Chair of Peter. Cardinal Bergoglio surely wanted reform in the Church and sought a holy successor to Benedict XVI, but that he should be elected pope? He did not see this coming. In humility, however, he stepped out on the balcony to the people, greeted them, and asked for their blessing. No man elected pope has all of the answers laid out before him as to what is going to occur after his election. A pope must resort to his advisors and must ultimately rely on the inspiration of the Holy Spirit to help guide him in guiding the Church of Christ.

This is a situation that every Christian experiences to a certain degree. Even when one makes the decision to dedicate one's life to Christ, the way is often imperfectly clear at first. This experience, however, goes a long way in keeping the Christian humble enough to recognize that he or she relies on God for spiritual progress. May the Holy Spirit always enlighten us so as to help us discern what we ought to do.

The First Franciscan Community

Accounts among St. Francis's biographers concerning the accruement of his first followers differ. Some, such as St. Bonaventure, suggest that he had quite a following before he went to Rome to seek the approval of Pope Innocent III for his way of life. According to Bonaventure, Francis had twelve followers, a highly symbolic number as the number of the twelve disciples of Christ, before he sought the papal blessing.

One of these initial followers, a priest in Assisi named Silvester, initially abhorred Francis's way of life, but then had a dream. As Bonaventure recounts,

> [Silvester] saw in a dream the whole town of Assisi encircled by a *huge dragon* (Dan. 14:22) which threatened to destroy the entire area by its enormous size. Then he saw coming from Francis's mouth a golden cross whose top touched heaven and whose arms stretched far and wide and seemed to extend to the ends of the world. At the sight of its shining splendor, the foul and hideous dragon was put to flight. (Bonaventure, *The Life of St. Francis*, III.5)

Upon having the dream three times, Silvester told Francis and his followers about the experience and began to follow the friars in their way of life.

It is said that Francis sent out his followers two by two, in accordance with the Gospel injunction (cf. Mk 6:7), to various places throughout Italy. Their home base was the Portiuncula, where they met together after these preaching missions. True to their rule, the friars followed a stringent way of life that included penance and charity. The purpose of these excursions was to preach penance to the people and to increase the numbers of the Franciscans, who were not called Franciscans at the time; instead, Francis told his brothers that they were to call themselves "penitents from Assisi." Taking no food, water, or extra clothes, they preached in various places, such as the Marches around Ancona and Florence. In fact, Bernard and Giles traveled as far away as France and Spain, visiting Santiago de Compestela. Wearing no shoes and enduring the cold, Bernard gave away his hood to a beggar. It took Bernard and Giles months to make the journey to Spain and back. Not knowing the language, Bernard and Giles could not preach to the people in these foreign lands and were often despised by the people.

These primitive excursions did not yield a large following, but they served as an excellent means for scouting out sites for future houses. In all of the places these early Franciscan friars visited, there are Franciscan sanctuaries today. The daring of these early Franciscans, and their willingness to risk all for the sake of Christ, planted the seeds for the future development of the Franciscan order.

On their way back from Rome, Francis and his companions took up residence in a dilapidated cowshed about forty miles north of the city. There they prayed and grew as a community. This humble abode sheltered the friars from the elements. Since they had no place to pray privately, Francis built a reed hut as an oratory. The friars prayed intensively in the morning and evenings. They listened to Bible readings, prayed the Lord's Prayer and the Hail Mary, and prayed from the Psalms. It is said that Francis prayed so intensely that one night, one of his brothers saw a fiery chariot rushing around the shed rafters. He at once notified the other friars, who all saw it and believed that it was the soul of Francis praying.

The preaching of Francis and his friars had a profound effect on the populace of Italy. They did not often receive permission to preach in churches, so they preached in the open air in the language of the people, rather than in Latin, which the people could not really understand. This contrasts with the practices of such saints as St. Bernard, who preached primarily in Latin to the educated. Francis, on the other hand, was dedicated to preaching the good news to the poor. The people were inspired by Francis's recounting of biblical scenes, such as the nativity or the crucifixion, and were entertained by his examples of morality and immortality from Arthurian romances. As a troubadour, Francis had acquired considerable storytelling skills and even a talent for entertainment. His enthusiasm brought about many kinds of reconciliation, including the reconciling of parish priests and parishioners, rich and poor, and many others of unequal social status. Francis taught people to view all others as their fellow brothers and sisters in Christ, and he inflamed many with the love of God.

Because of the success of their preaching, Francis and his companions attracted more followers. Eventually, Francis realized that the cowshed could not accommodate all of the friars and that they would have to find another place to stay. His prayers were answered when the Benedictines gave Francis and his companions the use of the Portiuncula as their headquarters. From there, the Franciscans would be able to preach penance to all and to multiply in numbers, ushering a myriad of souls into the kingdom of God through a life of penance, humility, poverty, and holiness.

Pope Innocent III expressed his hope that the Franciscan friars could serve as examples to his bishops and priests, who often liked to live in luxury and were frequently more concerned about their own comfort than the state of their flock. While Francis certainly set an example for the clergy, his preaching of penance had a profound impact on the common people. Likewise, the reformation of the Catholic Church today cannot be merely a reformation of the clergy; instead, all Catholics are called to follow in the footsteps of Christ. Jesus is calling all Catholics to enkindle within themselves, through the Holy Spirit, a newfound devotion to his Cross and to serving others. Without the conversion of heart among the people of God, Pope Francis's reform will not be successful. Now is the time when we need to open our hearts to God's grace; now is the time of salvation!

Life at the Portiuncula

St. Mary of the Angels, popularly called the Portiuncula, was a substantial gift to Francis and his companions. Francis loved this new place for a variety of reasons. The simplest reason for Francis's affection for this chapel was its dedication to the Blessed Virgin Mary. In medieval Europe, there was a burgeoning of Marian devotion. Francis had always associated Our Lady with poverty, and he maintained a dedicated devotion to her.

At the Portiuncula, Francis's companions grew in faith. Although these men were not highly educated, they learned about their faith through intense prayer and service. Their learning was acquired by studying not books but the Crucified. This disposition is reflected in St. Bonaventure's answer to St. Thomas Aquinas, his Dominican colleague at the University of Paris, who had asked the Franciscan where he had acquired his learning. In reply, Bonaventure pointed to a crucifix. This kind of learning was more closely aligned with pathos than with book learning as such, and Francis's companions grew considerably in this kind of knowledge and faith.

What were the friars' days like at the Portiuncula? Francis and his brothers prayed the Church's liturgical prayers, including the Mass, at which Francis would serve as deacon. Their senses were caught up in the Mass, and their prayers arose to God with the incense. After Mass, the brothers would perform their chores. Mindful of the importance of prayer, Francis made it a part of his Rule that the friars were not to speak from morning until noon. After noon, talk was not to be idle but, rather, to concern holy or necessary things. At the command of Francis, the friars would also go out and preach sermons at various churches in the area; and if they were invited anywhere, they would eat what was offered to them.

As the order grew, Francis acquired a keen insight as to the natures of those who intended to join his order. Occasionally, a rotten apple would slip past him, but he was always able to determine when this had happened. One man who expressed an interest in joining Francis had sold everything but then gave his money to his family instead of to the poor. When Francis found out, he dismissed this man from the order.

Masseo was tested by Francis to see if he was worthy of being allowed to stay in the order. Although Masseo had a remarkable ability to preach, Francis was concerned that this would make him prideful. Therefore, Francis assigned Masseo to such menial tasks as cooking and gatekeeping. Finally, his fellow friars protested, asking for a redistribution of the chores. All the while, Masseo kept silent and performed his duties obediently. This convinced Francis of his sincerity and his virtue. From that point on, Francis often chose Masseo as a companion and used him as a messenger.

What distinguished Francis and his companions from the Benedictines was the itinerancy and mendicant charism of the former. Rather than staying confined to one place, the Franciscans were often on the road, preaching to the people and serving the poor. In this sense, the Franciscans could be described as nomadic. Their travel was structured on a rotational basis; some of the friars were sent out to certain places to preach, whereas the other friars stayed at the Portiuncula to pray. Their style of preaching was not concerned with doctrine; instead, their focus was on encouraging people to embrace a life of penance and to rely on the sacraments. Francis and his companions eventually acquired some of the homiletic techniques that were in vogue at the time, but at first they preached simply the love of Jesus and the necessity to convert to the Lord. They always taught more by example than by their words. Through their itinerant nature, Francis and his companions were able to scatter the Word of God to the people, not in the form of a sophisticated exegesis but as living, walking icons of Jesus Christ. In Francis, people saw the face of Christ and a disciple who was wholly devoted to living the message that Jesus proclaimed.

The Franciscans were also a mendicant order. Instead of living off of endowments or tithes, as the Benedictines often did at the time, the friars grew their own food and often had to resort to begging for alms so that they could acquire enough sustenance. This aspect of their lives was something Francis insisted upon because of the radicalness of the Gospel injunction to give up everything and follow Christ. Ultimate poverty was Francis's goal, not for the sake of being poor but, rather, for the sake of following Christ as closely as possible. He firmly believed that by taking the leap of faith and doing what God asked of him and his companions, they would be provided for; and he was not disappointed.

All Christians are called to put on Christ by tenaciously fulfilling the demands of their baptism. We are all called to be Christ to others. This is a message that is just as true today as it was in thirteenth-century Italy. A Christian conversion comes about by living a life that is in conformity with Christ's, which allows people to begin seeing Christ alive in us. This is the kind of conversion Pope Francis wishes for the Church—a conversion that is capable of bringing about joy to people in today's somber world. Only by knowing and proclaiming Christ are Christians capable of reclaiming for themselves the joy that is rightfully theirs, a joy that stems from knowing they are loved by God.

The itinerant nature of the Franciscans was also a blessing since this initial impulse to spread the Gospel throughout the surrounding villages was a sign of greater things to come. In 1492 Christopher Columbus, a Secular Franciscan, sailed to the Americas. In 1493 Friar Juan Perez, a Franciscan, celebrated the first Mass in the New World. In the eighteenth century, Blessed Junípero Serra, O.F.M., set up multiple missions in California and was instrumental in the development of that portion of the present-day United States. The Franciscans played a vital role in the history of the Americas, a role they would not have been able to fulfill without the primary example of Francis and his followers. We will explore this theme further, later in the book. For the time being, we will continue the story of St. Francis himself.

Political and Religious Developments

At the Portiuncula, with its celestial architecture and peaceful aura, the friars certainly felt peace. During this time, however, the world was not so irenic. A crusade raged in the Holy Land. Otto, the new emperor, had a falling out with Pope Innocent III, and was ultimately excommunicated by him. In a fortuitous set of circumstances for Assisi, Otto moved against Perugia for supporting Philip of Swabia and the pope, so he had the prisoners from Assisi released from the Perugian prisons. Brothers and fathers were reunited with their families after years of imprisonment. Otto also forced Perugia and Assisi to make peace and oversaw the signing of a treaty at Assisi in 1210. The people of Assisi were elated at this fortuitous turn of events.

In addition to the upswing in the political state of affairs, there was a growing religious fervor. In 1212 the location of St. Rufino's relics was made known to a priest in a dream. After consulting with Bishop Guido, it was decided that the relics would be placed with great ceremony beneath the altar of the new cathedral. This led to many miracles and increased the esteem of the bishop in the eyes of the people.

In 1211 or 1212, Francis decided that he should travel to the Holy Land to seek peace between Christians and Muslims and thereby halt the bloodshed resulting from the Crusades, even if doing so meant that he would be martyred. With another friar, he went to the Adriatic coast and set sail on a ship toward the Orient, but a storm prevented them from reaching their destination. They arrived on the other side of the Adriatic instead. Unable to find a vessel willing to carry them, they stowed away on a ship, bringing with them a generous supply of food that someone had left them. When another storm broke out and the sailors began to run out of food, Francis and his companion shared their food with the sailors. The ship landed on the western coast of Italy, where Francis and his companion made his way home. Although his plan was thwarted this time, Francis would ultimately journey to the Holy Land in 1217.

When Francis arrived back at Assisi, many men and women were eager to follow his way of life. The women of the town and of the surrounding cities were impressed with Francis's genuineness, his love for the poor, and his desire to serve the people of God. Many sought his counsel. One woman sought his advice about her cantankerous relationship with her husband, who occasionally took to beating her. His response was that she should not worry but, instead, go home and strive for salvation with her husband. When she returned home, the two reconciled and lived the rest of their lives in celibacy, eventually dying on the same day. Their neighbors described the couple as saints.

Giacoma de Settesoli, one of the richest women in Italy at the time, assisted the friars. She contributed to the their good works and was present at Francis's death. After this event, she moved to Assisi, where her remains are kept partway down the stair to St. Francis's tomb. The eagerness of women to help Francis and his companions evokes images of women in the Gospel who contributed to the apostles' purse. Without the assistance of such women, Jesus' and Francis's respective ministries would not have been as successful as they were.

Women are extremely important in the Catholic Church, whether they are nuns, mothers, or single women. Through their affection, support, prayers, service, and generosity, women take a prime place in the cultivation of good works and in fostering the faith. Along with mothers, fathers share an obligation to hand on the faith to their children and to live as models of holiness for their children to emulate. This is all the more necessary today, when the family, the basic unit of society, is under attack.

According to Pope Francis, the role of women in Christianity is made most apparent in the mother of Jesus. In the pope's own words, "The woman has the gift of maternity, of tenderness; if all these riches are not integrated, a religious community not only transforms into a chauvinist society, but also into one that is austere, hard, and hardly sacred" (Bergoglio, 102). Women sustain the community through their sensitivity and their loving concern for all. There is a need for the feminine aspects of Christianity to be highlighted once again and for women to rediscover and embrace their feminineness.

In the pope's view, the philosophy of feminism, as characterized by radical feminists who insist on bridging the gap between the sexes, has failed to bring about true good to women. After the women's suffrage campaign of the 1920s, radical feminism attempted to draw battle lines between men and women. While Pope Francis insists that the philosophy of feminism does not benefit women, he is aware that women have "been the object of use, of profit, of slavery, and ... relegated to the background" (103). He calls this the work of Satan, who desires to crush the sources of life and salvation.

Pope Francis desires for men and women to recognize that masculinity and femininity are different but complementary and that there ought to be no gender-based power struggle in the Church. As Pope Francis notes, the mother of Jesus was greater than the apostles, but the ecclesiastical authority was passed on to men (102, 104). In *Evangelii Gaudium*, Pope Francis states, "The Church acknowledges the indispensable contribution which women make to society through the sensitivity, intuition and other distinctive skill sets which they, more than men, tend to possess. ... we need to create still broader opportunities for a more incisive female presence in the Church" (sec. 103).

May Mary, the mother of Christ, intercede for the Church, and may men and women everywhere open their hearts to the specific, engendered roles God has given them within the Church. Only through such an acceptance of the distinctions and respective grandeur of each of the sexes will Christians adequately support one another, and the role of the family be safeguarded.

Clare of Assisi, Part I: Choosing Christ

One of the women who followed St. Francis as a result of his growing renown was Clare of Assisi. Clare was born in either 1193 or 1194 to an aristocratic family. She grew up during a turbulent time; during Clare's childhood, Assisi was embroiled in the same local wars in which Francis engaged as a soldier. In fact, at the time of her birth, several houses next to her family home had been burned down.

Typically, aristocratic girls were brought up quietly, confined to the women's quarters as their families prepared them for marriage to a wealthy suitor. Little did Clare's family know that their daughter would become a great saint and cofounder of a religious order. According to the reports of her friends, Clare was a pious and modest child. She kept herself hidden whenever her family had male guests, and she saved her food so that it could be distributed to the poor. She was fond of romances and had a devotion to St. Agnes, who had rejected the suitors her family had wanted her to consider. Incidentally, one of her friends was named Ginevra, after Guinevere.

Having heard some of Francis's sermons on Sundays in 1210 or 1211, Clare became enamored of the poor man's message. She yearned to find out what impelled Francis to seek the way of life he did and why he had followed the words of Christ so literally. However, she faced a dilemma: since she was sixteen at the time, it would have been socially unacceptable for her to speak privately to Francis, who was in his late twenties by now. What was she to do? She had to act quickly since her family was pressing her to marry. Her case was made all the more urgent by her recent acquisition of a sizable dowry.

Somehow, a secret meeting was arranged between Clare and Francis. For the sake of propriety, Bona di Guelfuccio served as a chaperon to Clare while Brother Philip the Long accompanied Francis. A number of such clandestine meetings occurred, during which Francis urged Clare to embrace a life of penance. Ultimately, Clare was convinced that in order for her to fulfill God's plan for her, she would have to devote herself to Christ entirely as a nun. The question remained as to what kind of nun she would become.

Clare decided on a bold course of action, probably with the help of Francis and Bishop Guido. First, she gave her dowry away. Naturally, this upset Clare's family and her suitor, who still encouraged her to marry him. Despite the pressure from her family, she refused. Finally, on Palm Sunday in 1212, Clare received a palm branch from Bishop Guido, somehow bypassing the women's line. According to legend, this was a sign that had been established beforehand between Clare, Francis, and Bishop Guido. In the evening, Clare slipped out of her family's house through a secret passageway that was covered with bricks and beams. Obviously, Clare's family was not fond of the idea of their daughter entering a convent.

After she successfully snuck out of the house, Clare was met by a handful of people, including Francis, possibly another friar, and perhaps Pacifica, her mother's cousin. They went through the woods and made their way to the parish church, where Clare exchanged her gown for a simple habit, promised obedience to Francis, and made a vow of poverty. Francis cut her hair as a sign of his acceptance. Clare was finally a Franciscan, but she could not live with the Franciscan friars for several reasons. A woman living with friars would have been perceived as a scandal; and, moreover, her family could have found her easily if she had stayed with Francis and his brothers. For this reason, the decision was made that Clare would go to San Paulo delle Abbadesse at Bastia, which lay a short distance from Assisi.

When Clare's family found out that she had escaped and was at the Benedictine monastery, seven of them rode there to retrieve Clare. After several days of threatening and enticing her, they finally surrounded her in the chapel. Clare clung to the altar, but it was only when she showed them that her head had been shaved that they realized there was no hope of convincing her to return with them. After this, they left Clare.

Shortly after this, Francis moved Clare, Pacifica, and her sister Catherine, who had also been accepted into the order, to San Damiano. Thus was the first convent of Franciscan sisters established. This was also, perhaps, one of the last gifts of Bishop Guido to Francis, since the bishop died later that year.

Clare and her sisters needed a rule of life, which she requested that Francis compose for them. This rule proved similar to that which Francis had written for his brothers. Whenever anyone suggested that Clare become a "normal" nun by joining an abbey, she always replied that she had made her vow of obedience directly to Francis. Furthermore, her rule marked her as a Franciscan.

While some biographers report that something of a romance existed between Clare and Francis, nothing improper is apparent in their relationship. While it is true that they had many similarities, their mutual affection was based on their admiration for each other's devotion to Christ. For this reason, the friendship of Clare and Francis stands as a pure model of platonic friendship based on a common love of Christ. Clare admired Francis's devotion to Christ and was inspired by his particular form of imitating Christ; otherwise, she would not have eventually chosen that particular lifestyle. Nothing surprising in this is surprising since Christ is supremely attractive and all who follow him become as he is. This is why the saints shine in resplendence and why the saints have influenced so many others.

While their friendship lasted for as long as Francis lived, Clare and Francis hardly met after she was settled in San Damiano. They regularly corresponded, however, and their friendship and affection for each other never grew stale. What makes their love all the more edifying is that they were always true to their vows to Christ and never mistook the beauty of God himself for the beauty of the other person.

Clare of Assisi, Part II: A Holy Heroine

Throughout medieval Europe in the early thirteenth century, thousands of women were joining convents and religious orders. This often afforded women—especially those who were on the margins of society, such as the poor and the widows—a safe haven where they could be looked after. Of course, most of these nuns' intentions were spiritual rather than monetary, and they were overall sincere in their motives for joining these orders. In this cultural context, the women's branch of the Franciscan order experienced its initial burgeoning.

It is said that some six years before Clare joined the Franciscans and established the second order, Francis declared that San Damiano would be a house for holy women. Clare and her sisters therefore had a place to stay, and her group of companions slowly increased. Clare went on to outlive Francis by nearly three decades. Within her lifetime, she was able to see the spread of her communities over much of Europe. She advised popes and became known as a protector of Assisi. Clare's influence, which was influenced in turn by Francis's example, was nothing less than profound, and this rippling effect spread across the known world.

Clare's way of life was similar to that of the Franciscan friars in that both the men's and women's branches of the order were strictly devoted to a life of poverty. Therefore, they depended solely on almsgiving rather than on endowments, lands, or other typical sources of income to which other orders, such as the Benedictines, were accustomed. At the same time, Clare recognized early on that it would not be prudent for her sisters to beg in the streets for food as the friars did. As a result, they accepted food if it was offered, but they primarily stayed in their convents. Francis therefore arranged for two friars to beg for food on behalf of Clare and her sisters. This way, Clare and her companions could remain true to their vow of poverty and live a true mendicant lifestyle while avoiding danger and scandal.

Clare and her companions lived a simple life. They met several times a day for prayer. Silvester and Leo, two Franciscan friars, heard the sisters' confessions and said Mass for them. Clare kept her sisters busy by directing them to make their own habits, grow fruits and vegetables, and help out their neighbors. The simplicity of their way of life must have struck a chord with many of the women in Assisi and its environs. Within several years, over fifty companions joined Clare. Soon after this, with the establishment of other convents, their numbers grew into the hundreds.

At the end of Clare's life of prayer and penance, a dozen of the original members of her order testified to her sanctity, including her sisters Agnes and Beatrice, her cousins Balvina and Amata, Pacifica, Benvenuta, Christina di Bernardo, and Agenese di Oportulo. Clare's companions offered strong testimony to her holiness. In one account, Pacifica described how Clare often healed the sisters simply by praying and making the sign of the cross. Benvenuta described Clare's bravery when Arab mercenaries had scaled the convent walls.

G. K. Chesterton observes that if Clare had eloped instead of running away from her home to become a nun, the modern world would regard her as a heroine. At the same time, she is to be considered among the greatest women in the history because of her bravery, sanctity, and determination. Chesterton also defends Clare's early decision to run away from home, observing that at that particular time in history, girls were married at an early age and teenagers often went to war, started businesses, and made other adult decisions. Therefore, at seventeen, Clare was certainly capable of making the decision to join an order. Having made this choice, Clare became a source of inspiration to thousands of others who followed in her wake. Of course, all of this was due to her connection to Francis and, ultimately, due to Francis's particular imitation of Christ.

The chaste friendship of Clare and Francis remains one of the most remarkable friendships in the history of Christianity. Dante and Beatrice, John of the Cross and Teresa of Avila, Francis and Clare—these spiritual couples, so to speak, complemented each other in remarkable ways. In fact, it is almost impossible to mention one without the other, so intertwined were the lives of these individuals. Francis looked upon Clare as a daughter and a confidant, as a disciple and as a unique spiritual contributor to the direction of the Franciscan movement since only she could directly watch over the women in her community day in and day out. Clare made Francis's way of life accessible to women as well as to men, thereby opening up the Franciscan movement to both genders.

What about those people who lived in the world, however? Would they be barred from following the Franciscan way of life? The next chapter explores the origins of the Secular

Franciscan Order. With the establishment of this lay order, the Franciscan triumvirate of orders would be complete.

The Third Order of Franciscans

In Cannara, a village approximately six miles south of Assisi, Francis preached a sermon on penance that so impressed the villagers that everyone wanted to leave and follow him. Surprised, Francis told the villagers to be patient and that he would let them know the best way for them to be saved. This was the beginning of the Secular Franciscan Order.

Francis's advocate, Cardinal Ugolino (later to become Pope Gregory IX), aided Francis in composing of the rule of the Third Order. Thereafter, men and women, regardless of their stations, could join the Franciscan movement by living in the world and infusing it with the Franciscan charism. They took vows and met together frequently to pray, but they also continued to perform the daily duties attendant to their respective states of life. By 1215, many men and women were associated with Francis's movement by way of belonging to the First, Second, or Third order.

There are no written records of this earliest period of the Third Order of Franciscans, who at that time were simply called the Brothers and Sisters of Penance. We know that there were many followers of Francis from all walks of life. Francis urged them to honor the church, go to confession regularly, attend Mass, respect the clergy, love their neighbors and enemies, give alms, be abstemious, and avoid sin.

Some of Francis's most valuable contributions came from early tertiaries. The wealthy count Orlando of Chiusi donated Francis Mt. LaVerna as a retreat site in 1213. At Mt. LaVerna, Francis would receive his vision of the seraph and, eleven years later, the stigmata. Giovanni di Velita gave Francis a sanctuary at Greccio. There many tertiaries gathered to pray psalms and hymns. The number of tertiaries soon numbered in the hundreds, if not thousands. The influence of the Third Order rapidly became apparent.

In addition to the influence that the Third Order of Franciscans exerted during the time of St. Francis, they have since had a profound impact on world history. There is a long list of renowned secular Franciscans, including popes, cardinals, royalty, adventurers, writers, artists, musicians, and scientists.

Among famous popes, Pius IX, Leo XIII, St. Pius X, Bl. Pius XII, and St. John XXIII were secular Franciscans. Pius IX is known for having put the seal on the doctrines of papal infallibility and the Immaculate Conception, whereas Leo XIII is known for his social encyclicals and devotion to Our Lady. Of course, St. John XXIII was known as the pope who began the Second Vatican Council and was canonized (along with St. John Paul II) on April 27, 2014. St. Charles Borromeo, a cardinal, was also a secular Franciscan.

There have also been royal members of the Secular Franciscans, including St. Louis IX, St. Elizabeth of Hungary, St. Elizabeth of Portugal, and Ferdinand and Isabella of Spain. Speaking of the latter, Christopher Columbus too was a secular Franciscan, as was Vasco de Gama. St. Joan of Arc was also a Franciscan tertiary. These leaders and explorers did much to advance the modern world and to institute justice for all people, especially the poor. Without Ferdinand and Isabella, Columbus could not have set out on his world-changing quest.

Dante Alighieri, the famous Italian poet who wrote the *Divine Comedy*, was a Franciscan tertiary, as was Miguel Cervantes, the author of *Don Quixote*. Giotto di Bondone, the Florentine painter who portrayed the life of Francis in paintings, was another secular Franciscan; so were Leonardo da Vinci, Raphael, and Michelangelo, the great Renaissance artists. Giovanni Pierluigi da Palestrina, the talented composer of sacred polyphony; Franz Liszt, the debonair pianist and composer; and, in our own times, John Michael Talbot are all associated with the Secular Franciscans. Some of the greatest artists who have ever lived were devotees of Francis's way of life and desired to emulate the ideals of the poor man of Assisi. Francis's aesthetic sensibilities, manifested in his love of nature and his appreciation of all God's creation, as well as his love of God through his imitation of Christ, inspired numerous artists in his wake. Francis of Assisi has thereby inspired some of the greatest works of art and literature the world has ever seen.

In addition to those Secular Franciscans who were associated with the humanities, a number of scientists were Franciscan tertiaries. These Franciscan scientists included Galileo Galilei, the great astronomer and inventor of the telescope; André-Marie Ampère and Luigi Galvani, who were instrumental in the field of electricity and electromagnetism; and Louis Pasteur, who saved countless lives through his work on vaccinations. Without these scientists, the world as we know it would not exist. Obviously, nothing in the spiritual vision of Francis would impede learning or knowledge. Although Francis exhorted his brothers to be simple and not to seek learning for its own sake, the vocation of the tertiaries to follow their own callings and occupations in this world allowed for these scientists to foster their faith and their scientific work simultaneously, thereby bringing much benefit to humanity by way of electrical and medical technology.

This impressive list demonstrates just how influential the Secular Franciscan Order has been since St. Francis's life. For many great leaders, artists, scientists, and other visionaries, devotion to Christ in the form of a Franciscan lifestyle was the religious inspiration behind their lives and work.

Francis's Encounter with the Sultan

Once Francis had settled Clare and her sisters and had established the Brothers and Sisters of Penance, he decided that it was time for him to preach to the Sultan in hopes of brokering a peace between Muslims and Christians. Bonaventure and Thomas of Celano insist that Francis was bent on martyrdom. This is perhaps overly dramatic since Francis's primary intentions were to speak to the Muslim leader, preach the Gospel, and bring about peace between Christians and Muslims—although, if this meant that he would have to die for his faith, then so be it.

Francis set out in 1219 and sailed to Acre in the summertime with perhaps ten or eleven friars. One story has Francis letting a child choose which friars would go, since the captain would not accept more than a dozen because of a lack of space. When Francis reached the Crusader camp, he found a motley crew of warriors, including knights as well as common foot soldiers. The Crusaders made their way to Damietta, a city on the delta of the Nile in Egypt. At some point, either before or after the Christian victory over Damietta, Francis went to speak to Malik-al-Kamil, the caliph, with Brother Illuminato. They were in danger of death since there were bounties for the heads of Christians. When the soldiers realized that Francis was no threat and that the friars, who looked like madmen, might prove entertaining to the sultan, they brought them to al-Kamil.

Once in the presence of the sultan, Francis was graciously received, and he was allowed to spend a few days preaching to the sultan's court. Some accounts have Francis offering to endure a trial by fire if a Muslim in the court were willing to do the same, to prove the relative veracity of their respective faiths, but the sultan refused. There is no reason to think that Francis was mad for making such an offer. As Chesterton noted, "Indeed throwing himself into the fire was hardly more desperate, in any case, than throwing himself among the weapons and tools of torture of a horde of fanatical Muhammadans and asking them to renounce Muhammad" (102).

There are those who believe that Malik-al-Kamil was a member of the Sufi brotherhood, which emphasized union with Allah through love. If this was the case, and he was in fact a mystic, it would help explain why Francis was not treated with contempt and ignominy. Something more than Francis's unassuming appearance, derived from his beggar's clothes, seemingly made an impression upon the sultan. Francis preached to the sultan and to his theological experts, who unanimously declared that Francis and Illuminato were dangerous and that the sultan should behead them immediately for tempting them all to commit apostasy. Of course, the sultan did no such thing. Instead, he listened patiently to what Francis had to say. When they were done speaking, the sultan explained that it was impossible for him to convert but asked Francis to pray for him and to ask God that he would show him the true faith before he died. He then offered Francis and Illuminato a treasure, which Francis refused. Instead, he accepted a sumptuous meal that the sultan provided, and the brothers were then escorted back to the crusader lines.

This encounter had a profound spiritual significance. Francis made a favorable impression on the clerics from Acre, some of whom became Franciscans. Moreover, Francis had attempted something no other Christian had done: to approach a Muslim with the Christian faith, without bearing arms. His outreach to Muslims occurred during a time when five of his brothers were martyred in Morocco, where they had preached the Gospel of Christ, an event that inspired St. Anthony of Padua to join the Franciscans.

Risking his own life to preach the Gospel and bring about peace, Francis demonstrated missionary zeal and a willingness to accomplish great things through his Christian courage, which eventually led to Franciscan custody of the Holy Land. In 1229 the Franciscan friars had a house near the fifth station on the Via Dolorosa. In 1309 they settled in the Holy Sepulcher and Bethlehem. Finally, in 1342, Pope Clement VI decreed that the Franciscans would be the official custodians of the sacred sites for the Catholic Church. This custody over the Holy Land still exists today, as the Franciscans have maintained a presence in the Middle East over the centuries. There is a nearly ubiquitous presence of Franciscan friars at the holy places of Jesus' life, death, and resurrection.

In today's world, as in Francis's, Islam is a force to be reckoned with. Since September 11, 2001, the dangers of radical Islam have become apparent to the entire Western world. The imperative to preach the Gospel has not lessened since the time of Francis, although in our contemporary world, an emphasis is placed on interreligious dialogue. Francis's desire to bring about peace and his zeal to save souls must be rekindled in the Church today.

Pope Francis recently traveled to the Holy Land in company with a rabbi and an imam. This symbolic gesture represented Pope Francis's dedication to peace, religious tolerance, and openness to people of different views. At the same time, the pope called on Muslims not to offend the name of God by committing violence in God's name. Christians must stand firm in their faith; they must respect Muslims but also preach to them through the example of extraordinarily holy lives. Only by following the path of Christ will the peace that this world so desperately needs become a reality.

St. Francis's Love of Nature

Augustine Thompson, O.P., a recent biographer of St. Francis of Assisi, describes Francis's love of nature as follows:

> Francis felt a deep union with living creatures, who, like the lilies of the field and the birds of the air, lived the Gospel precept of complete reliance on God spontaneously and naturally ... they followed the Gospel of complete reliance on God better than some of Francis's followers. Here was a "religious community" that needed no leader and no correction. No wonder Francis felt a union with them. (54)

Francis's love of nature is made evident by the legends that surround his interaction with animals. Once he found a cricket at the Portiuncula and asked it to sing its praises to God. Every day for a week, the cricket would sit on his finger and sing for him for an hour, until he gave it permission to leave. On another occasion, he walked into the middle of a flock of birds and told them to praise God. They began to open their wings and sing, which delighted Francis greatly. This theme of creation praising God is a powerful image, for it highlights the unity that exists among all God's creatures.

In addition to his love for creation, Francis had a soft spot for animals that were in danger of being killed for food, even if it was intended for Francis and his brothers. Once, when a brother had caught a hare to feed the community, Francis petted the animal and let it go out of compassion. Francis had a special affection for lambs in particular since they reminded him of Christ, the Lamb of God. Seeing a couple of lambs being carried to the slaughter by a shepherd, he convinced the shepherd to trade them for his cloak. Francis liked larks above all other animals because they reminded him of his Franciscan brothers, with their beautiful singing and their habits like the lark's feathers. His love of animals was so great that he cared for the worms by moving them out of the road so that they would not get crushed.

A wolf once terrorized the villagers of Gubbio. Francis approached and rebuked the wolf, but he recognized that it attacked the villagers' animals because it was hungry. He made a pact between the wolf and the people, telling the villagers that if they promised to feed the wolf, it would not attack them or their animals. The villagers agreed, surprised to see the wolf acting so benignly toward Francis—even shaking Francis's hand with its paw. After two years, the wolf died, and the villagers buried him in their church. Indeed, beneath the chapel of San Francesco della Pace, a skeleton of a wolf was excavated in 1872.

Francis's relationship with nature is easily romanticized. While he loved creatures, however, he also described a bird that had drowned as cursed and believed that some pests were sent by the devil to make him suffer. He did not like flies, and whenever a brother did not work, Francis was wont to call him Brother Fly. He playfully referred to his stubborn body, which he attempted to tame and rule, as Brother Ass.

Although Francis loved creatures dearly, he was not a vegetarian. He followed the Gospel rule that permitted disciples of Christ to eat meat. Nor was Francis pantheistic; rather, he recognized clearly that creatures came from God but were not God himself. Francis always distinguished between the Godhead and the rest of creation. However, he did somehow narrow the gap that existed in the medieval mind between human beings and animals—by associating with them, speaking to them, asking them to praise God, and emphasizing the common creator of both humans and beasts.

In addition to his affinity for animals, Francis loved all of creation. He loved flowers and cared for trees. In fact, he would ask the brother who was in charge of cutting wood to be sure to leave enough trees that they would grow again. His love of all creation is perhaps best expressed in his "Canticle to Brother Sun," which he composed shortly before he died:

Most High, all-powerful, good Lord,
Yours are the praises, the glory, the honor, and
all blessing.
To You alone, Most High, do they belong,
and no man is worthy to mention Your name.
Praised be You, my Lord, with all your creatures,
especially Sir Brother Sun,
Who is the day and through whom You give us
light.
And he is beautiful and radiant with great
splendor;
and bears a likeness of You, Most High One.
Praised be You, my Lord, through Sister Moon
and the stars,
in heaven You formed them clear and precious
and beautiful.
Praised be You, my Lord, through Brother Wind,
and through the air, cloudy and serene, and
every kind of weather

through which You give sustenance to Your
creatures.
Praised be You, my Lord, through Sister Water,
which is very useful and humble and precious
and chaste.
Praised be You, my Lord, through Brother Fire,
through whom You light the night
and he is beautiful and playful and robust and
strong.
Praised be You, my Lord, through our Sister
Mother Earth,
who sustains and governs us,
and who produces varied fruits with colored
flowers and herbs.
Praised be You, my Lord, through those who give
pardon for Your love
and bear infirmity and tribulation.
Blessed are those who endure in peace
for by You, Most High, they shall be crowned.
Praised be You, my Lord, through our Sister
Bodily Death,
from whom no living man can escape.
Woe to those who die in mortal sin.
Blessed are those whom death will find in Your

most holy will,

for the second death shall do them no harm.

Praise and bless my Lord and give Him thanks

and serve Him with great humility.

(*Francis and Clare: The Complete Works*, 38-39)

This poem, as simple as it is profound and as plain as it is beautiful, supposedly inspired Dante to write his *Divine Comedy* in Italian instead of Latin. To this day, "Canticle to Brother Sun" is the oldest surviving piece of poetry written in Italian.

In 1979, Pope John Paul II declared St. Francis of Assisi to be the patron saint of ecology. A large part of the legacy that Francis bequeathed to later generations was his example of harmony with creation. Instead of setting themselves over and against creation, and perceiving plants, animals, and the earth as mere objects to exploit, human beings should care for the created world. Francis, who made a habit of calling animals his brothers and sisters, displayed a connection with nature, and sensitivity toward all of creation, that the modern world would do well to emulate.

The Stigmata

Toward the end of Francis's life on earth, in the fall of 1224, he had a mystical experience while on retreat at Mount LaVerna. Before this incident, Pacifico, one of Francis's companions, had a vision in which he saw a row of thrones in heaven. One of the thrones, which stood higher and was more ornate than all the others, sat empty. When Pacifico asked whose throne this was, the reply came that it had been Lucifer's but would now belong to Francis since what Lucifer had lost by pride, Francis gained by his humility. In accordance with his special devotion to St. Michael the Archangel, Francis decided to precede the feast of St. Michael in 1224 with a forty-day fast on Mount LaVerna. He went with a small group of friars and made his way up the mountain, where he prayed for some weeks with his brothers.

On the feast of the Exaltation of the Cross, September 14, when Francis was engaged in deep meditation, a seraph (see Isa 6:2) appeared to Francis in a vision. Rays that emanated from the seraph pierced Francis's hands, feet, and side, thus leaving the impression of Christ's wounds upon his body. This profound mystical experience left an indelible mark not only upon Francis but also upon the history of the world. Never before had the wounds of Christ appeared so obviously on one of his followers. In fact, Francis's stigmata represented the first documented case of this phenomenon.

Thomas of Celano, one of Francis's earliest biographers, describes the stigmata in the following words:

> He was in a vision a Seraph upon a cross, having six wings, extended above him, arms and feet affixed to a cross. *Two of his wings were raised up over his head, two were stretched out as if for flight,* and *two covered his whole body.* Seeing this, he was filled with the greatest awe, but as he did not know what this vision meant for him, joy mixed with sorrow flooded his heart. He greatly rejoiced at the gracious look that he saw the Seraph gave him, but the fact that it was fixed to the cross terrified him. With concern his mind pondered what this revelation could mean, and the search for some meaning made his spirit anxious. But understanding came from discovery: while he was searching outside himself, the meaning was shown to him in his very self. At once signs of the nails began to appear on his hands and feet, just as he had seen

them a little while earlier on the crucified man in the air over him ... His right side was marked with an oblong red scar as if pierced by a lance. (320-321)

This dramatic encounter with a celestial being made a lasting impression not only on Francis but also on his brothers. This impact, however, was not far-reaching until after his death, when his stigmata were revealed to all. Francis only told his closest brothers at Mount LaVerna, including Brother Illuminato, about what had happened, saying that he was told secrets he must not repeat to anyone. Try as he might, however, Francis was unable to conceal his stigmata from everyone since he was already such a popular religious figure.

In Bonaventure's classic account of this event, after Francis received the stigmata, the hailstorms that had so often plagued the vicinity of Mount LaVerna ceased, much to the amazement of the people who lived in the area. Instead, the sun shone, and all of nature was serene. In addition to this meteorological miracle, Bonaventure attributes a number of miraculous cures to Francis's stigmata. On one occasion, Francis touched a poor man who had trouble sleeping in the cold; at once, the man felt a marvelous heat and fell into a deep sleep. Another time, a plague had broken out among the sheep and cattle in Rieti. A man was given a vision to fetch water in which Francis had washed his hands and feet and to sprinkle it on the animals. As soon as the water touched the animals, they recovered.

For the last two years of his life, Francis carried on his person the wounds of Christ. Many people, including Pope Alexander IV, testified to seeing Francis's stigmata while he was still alive. Despite Francis's best efforts, he could not conceal his stigmata from everyone. The wound in his side, especially, caused him great pain, particularly when someone touched it accidentally.

St. Bonaventure's interpretation of Francis's vision is that he received it so that "he might learn in advance that he was to be totally transformed into the likeness of Christ crucified, not by the martyrdom of his flesh, but by the fire of his love consuming his soul" (Bonaventure, 306). In Bonaventure's mystical theology, the six wings of the seraph "symbolize the six steps of illumination that begin from creatures and lead up to God, whom no one rightly enters except through the Crucified" (55). This is the structuring motif behind

Bonaventure's *Itinerarium Mentis ad Deum*, or *The Soul's Journey into God*.

What is the meaning of the stigmata for us today? Firstly, they are a reminder of the love Christians should have for Jesus Christ, who was crucified for our sins. They are also a reminder that we should have the passion of Our Lord always before our minds. Christ's wounds express the remarkable love God has for humanity and the gratitude we owe him for his many gifts to us, the most important of which is the gift of salvation. The merits of Jesus' sufferings continue to apply to Christians today. Although he is no longer hanging on the Cross but, rather, is seated at the right hand of God the Father, he still extends his arms over the world. From his throne in heaven, our high priest raises his pierced hands in prayer over the world, interceding for his people until we are made perfect. For this to occur, however, we need to cooperate with the grace that God offers us. He wishes that we would be made perfect, but how few are those who courageously relinquish all else to follow him! The stigmata of St. Francis are a reminder of God's infinite love and of Jesus' triumph over death, in which we are called to share.

Lady Poverty

Francis described poverty as "the special way to salvation" (Bonaventure, 240). He longed for poverty with all his heart and desired to be the poorest person for the sake of Christ. He fully embraced the Gospel ideal of selling one's possessions and giving them to the poor, and he made this a requirement of entering the order. Whenever he saw someone dressed more poorly than himself, he would rebuke himself and strive to be poorer than the person he had encountered. Francis would not leave the poor person and then strive to be poor by his own means, however; far from this, Francis saw in the faces of the poor an image of Christ himself, to be imitated by grace. According to Bonaventure, Francis told his fellow friars, "When you see a poor man, my brother, an image of the Lord and his poor mother is being placed before you. Likewise in the case of the sick, consider the physical weakness which the Lord took upon himself" (Bonaventure, 254).

Francis tended to the needs of the poor and would even give away his own necessities, which others had given to him. Bonaventure recounts that Francis also took upon his shoulders the heavy loads of poor people so that they would not have to carry the burdens themselves. Francis's compassion shone in all he did, especially in his relationship with the poor. On one occasion, Francis gave away his clothes to a beggar woman, who ran away with them. Finding that she did not have enough cloth to make a dress out of them, she went back and told Francis. He therefore asked his companion to give his clothes to the woman as well, ensuring that the woman would now have enough material.

The friars' eating habits were extremely austere. They often squatted on the ground as they ate. The food they prepared often consisted of scraps of meat, some vegetables, and bread crusts. Whenever a brother soaked beans overnight, Francis would rebuke him since they had taken vows not to have any concerns for tomorrow. Francis was not an ascetic for the sake of increasing his and his brothers' pain but out of his love for Christ. His intention was not to make the brothers suffer; if that had been the case, then he would not have given the best food to the friars who were elderly and sick. When Silvester was ill, for instance, Francis gave him the best grapes from the vineyard before the other brothers awoke. This anecdote reveals that although Francis was an ascetic, he did not revel in pain; rather, he accepted suffering out of love for his crucified Lord.

What was the inspiration for Francis's poverty? Put simply, it was his desire to imitate Christ as closely as possible. He saw

Christ's life as one of voluntary poverty that thereby enabled others to become rich. Jesus was born in a manger, had no place to rest his head, and was ultimately executed as a criminal. Francis did not want to be provided for. He did not want to join a monastery where he would have all of the food, clothing, and goods that he would ever need. He wanted to know what it was like to be truly poor, to be a poor person living in the world and to rely on the good will of others for his daily sustenance. Francis wanted to beg for his food, and he wanted nothing in this world to call his own. He wanted only to be like Jesus. For this reason, Francis's vision of poverty was strikingly different from the monastic view of poverty as common possession. Francis, rather, wanted to have no possessions whatsoever.

Francis was so enamored of poverty and so inspired by this Gospel ideal that, according to Bonaventure, Francis called poverty "his mother, his bride, and his lady" (244). He referred to poverty as Lady Poverty and told his friars to "love and be faithful to our Lady Holy Poverty" (*Francis and Clare*, 164). In Francis's vision, Our Lady and poverty are especially linked. Not only was Mary poor, like Jesus, but she was also the exemplar of all the virtues because she was free from all sin and perfectly obedient to Christ. This outlook reflects the doctrine of the Immaculate Conception, which was defended by the Franciscan theologian Bl. Duns Scotus and proclaimed a dogma by Pius IX in 1854. In "The Salutation to the Virtues," which was sometimes called "The virtues possessed by the holy Virgin, and which should be present in a holy soul," Francis addresses the virtue of poverty as follows: "Lady, holy Poverty, may the Lord protect you with your sister, holy Humility" (*Francis and Clare*, 151). This beautiful salutation demonstrates how closely Francis connected poverty with the Blessed Virgin Mary.

For Francis, poverty was a way of sharing in the poverty of the holy family. It was his way of participating in the family of God, relying only on God the Father for his temporal well-being while imitating his Lord Jesus and Our Lady, whom he found to be an indispensable spiritual advocate. It was for this reason that he entrusted his order to her care.

The Death of Francis

In 1225 and 1226, toward the end of Francis's life on earth, he endured a variety of physical ailments. He already suffered from the excruciating pain of the stigmata, by which he was conformed to the Cross of Christ; now, he would suffer near-blindness, malnutrition, and malaria. In the spring of 1225, Francis went to say his farewell to Clare; but Clare, cognizant of Francis's physical ailments, insisted that he stay with her near San Damiano so that his friars could look after him. She had a house of reeds constructed and attached to the church. There Francis was tormented by sunlight and could not read by candlelight. He could not receive eye surgery right away since it wasn't the proper season; he would have to wait. Francis lived in this hut for almost two months. During this time, Francis composed the "Canticle to Brother Sun." As Augustine Thompson remarks, in this canticle Francis paid homage to the sun, which caused him his greatest pain (123).

In the summer, Francis left Assisi for Rieti to acquire medical treatment for his eyes. His brothers found it difficult to care for him. Although Francis had allowed his fellow friars to eat choice food when they were sick, he refused to eat the best food during his own sickness. He even declined to hear the reading of Scripture, saying that he recalled enough Scripture and could meditate on many verses. He also quoted David, who said that his soul refused to be consoled. For these reasons, Francis proved a difficult patient.

Finally, Francis consulted with a doctor who decided that the best course of action would be to cauterize Francis's flesh from his jaw to the eyebrow of his bad eye. This operation was performed, but it did not have the desired effect of stopping the flow from Francis's eyes. Another doctor recommended that his ears be pierced. This was done as well, also to no avail. The only thing Francis could do now was to recover from his surgeries. Afterward he received medical attention at Siena, but this did not help him much, either.

One evening Francis started to vomit blood, which could have been a result of a stomach ulcer or stomach cancer. Francis began to prepare his brothers for his death and for life in the Franciscan order without him. Brother Elias heard of this and asked Francis to compose a last testament for the brothers.

Finally, in July or August of 1226, Francis returned to Assisi with an escort of armed knights since the people of Assisi feared that he would die in a foreign city. The people of Assisi, who had formerly believed that Francis was a madman, now honored him as a saint even before he died. They placed him in the bishop's house and had an armed guard posted in front of his quarters at night. Although Francis was nearly blind, he was still able to appreciate music, so he asked that the brothers sing hymns of praise. The doctor who assessed Francis at this time told him that he did not have long to live and that he would die between the end of September and October 4.

The friars carried Francis to the Portiuncula on a litter so that they could honor his wish to die there, the place where his order first grew. He blessed Assisi as he left it. When he arrived at the Portiuncula, he called on Giacoma and sent word to Clare. He left his last testament with the brothers and asked them to sprinkle his body with ashes once he died and to say psalms over his dead body. One evening before his death, he could not sleep because of the pain he endured. The next morning, he took bread and had it broken and distributed to the friars who were present. He then blessed the friars and asked them to keep in their prayers all those who had been in their order, were currently in their order, or who would join their order in the future.

Only a few days later, Francis passed. Immediately beforehand, he asked that the passion according to the Gospel of John be read to him. According to Bonaventure, one of the friars saw Francis's soul ascending into heaven in the form of a bright star. It was also reported that larks gathered in a great multitude over the place where Francis lay and that they sang when he died. This sign was fitting since the sight of them filled him with joy and he had so often invited them to praise God.

Before he died, Francis asked the friars to assist him with one last act of humility: he wanted his body stripped of all of his clothes after his death and left in this state for as long as it takes a man to walk a mile, which is approximately thirty minutes. The friars honored Francis's request. Francis was naked when he came into the world and naked after he departed. So committed to poverty was Francis that, at the end of his life, he wanted nothing attached to his body. After the prescribed period of time, Francis's body was clothed in a gray habit. At his death, the miracle of his stigmata was made known to all who were present.

In 1228, two years after Francis's death, Pope Gregory IX declared Francis a saint. This pope was closely connected to the Franciscans. He wrote the rule for the Poor Clares and also heavily influenced the rule of the Secular Franciscans. For a long time, he had been the cardinal protector of the order, and he personally knew Francis. Since Francis died just after the sun had set on October 3, his feast day was declared October 4, for in the medieval period, the commencement of the new day was recognized at sundown.

Francis's death serves as a model for all Christians to follow. He left the world stripped of every worldly desire, and he focused on the passion of his Lord as he was dying. Francis's death, however, was made all the more pure and holy since he had prepared for it throughout so much of his life by his great devotion to Jesus Christ crucified.

The example he offered to his followers had a ripple effect that impacted the rest of history. This is evident in one of Francis's great disciples, St. Anthony of Padua, who is the subject of the next chapter. Following this is an investigation of the Franciscans' impact on the New World. Thereafter, over the course of two chapters, Francis's legacy on Pope Francis will be analyzed. The final chapter addresses the importance of St. Francis of Assisi for our time.

St. Anthony of Padua

One of the most famous Franciscan saints in history is St. Anthony of Padua, a Portuguese priest who became associated with Padua after he moved to Italy. His birth name was Fernando Martins de Bulhões, and he was born in 1195 in Lisbon. He hailed from a wealthy family and joined the Augustinians at the age of 15. He learned Latin and theology and became an expert in Scripture. After being ordained a priest, he encountered some Franciscan friars who eventually settled in a hermitage near the Augustinians. Fernando was drawn to their lifestyle. When he heard that some of the Franciscan friars who had gone to preach the Gospel in Morocco had been martyred for the faith, he decided that he wanted to become a Franciscan. He obtained permission to leave the Augustinians so that he could become a Franciscan, and they acquiesced.

Fernando took the name Anthony after joining the Franciscans, after the name of the hermitage of the Franciscans he had first met. Anthony set out for Morocco but had to return to Portugal; the ship he was on, however, was blown off course and brought him to Sicily. He eventually settled in a Franciscan convent in Tuscany. In 1222 a group of Dominicans came to town, but they were unprepared to give a sermon. Therefore, Anthony was called upon to deliver the sermon. Although he was unprepared, he gave a sermon of such brilliance that it left a lasting impression on all who heard him.

Soon afterward, he came to the attention of St. Francis. Although Francis did not want his brothers to be immersed in books or overly concerned with theological arguments, he recognized the necessity of having a theologian in their midst so that those Franciscan friars who had a calling to the priesthood could acquire the necessary theological training. Francis found that Anthony truly loved the Franciscan charism and that his skill as a theologian did not detract from his simplicity, genuineness, and humility. In 1224 Francis put Anthony in charge of teaching all the friars who went on to pursue theological studies. According to Benedict XVI, "Anthony laid the foundations of Franciscan theology which ... was to reach its apex with St Bonaventure of Bagnoregio and Bl. Duns Scotus."

While Anthony was a masterful theologian, he was better known as a preacher. Anthony primarily preached in France and Italy, and his sermons always proved edifying to his listeners. He inspired people to turn away from sin, and criminals would reform upon hearing him preach about the mercy of Christ. Pope Gregory IX referred to him as the Ark of the Testament, and his preaching was described as a "jewel case of the Bible." His preaching ability was renowned throughout much of Europe. His methods included the use of allegory and the explanation of Scripture in symbolic terms. Anthony bequeathed to the church two sets of sermons: "Sunday Sermons" and "Sermons on the Saints." These two collections of sermons were to be used by Franciscan preachers. The richness of his sermons is so great that Pope Pius XII declared St. Anthony a Doctor of the Church.

Exhausted from his missionary journeys and having contracted ergotism, Anthony went with two other friars to a retreat at Camposampiero, a village about twelve miles north of Padua, to get some rest. On their way back, Anthony died at the age of 35 on June 13, 1231, just outside the gates of Padua. He was buried in Padua and quickly became the patron saint of the town. In fact, his canonization process was so swift— the second quickest canonization in the history of the Catholic Church—that he was canonized less than a year after his death.

In art, Anthony is depicted with either a lily or the child Jesus. This latter symbol is derived from several stories wherein

Anthony was seen praying in his room, warmly holding the infant Jesus in his arms. He is also known as the patron saint of lost objects. Many Catholics ask St. Anthony to intercede for them when they lose their keys or other objects of importance. The reason for this is that once, when a collection of Anthony's sermon notes was stolen from him, he prayed to God that he might reacquire his book, and the thief, experiencing contrition, returned the book. In some cultures, Anthony is the patron saint of marriages as well since it was said that he reconciled couples.

St. Anthony of Padua was known also as the "Wonder Worker," both during his life and afterward, because of the many miracles attributed to him. In addition to his vast popularity as a miracle worker, he also stands as a prime example of a humble theologian, providing Bonaventure and Duns Scotus a distinctly Franciscan theological basis. Furthermore, Anthony was known as a friend of the poor because of his love for those who lacked worldly wealth. Overall, he exemplified a man who was remarkably influenced by the Franciscan spirit—who united his own talents with the evangelical way of life of St. Francis of Assisi. His charity, fidelity to the Gospel, and humility, which reflect Francis's, have contributed to his popularity among all God's people.

May St. Anthony of Padua pray for us today as we strive to follow the will of God in our lives.

The Franciscan Impact on the New World

As previously mentioned, King Ferdinand and Queen Isabella of Spain, as well as Christopher Columbus, were Third Order Franciscans. The Franciscans were also one of the largest religious orders in Europe at the time. In fact, one estimate places the number of Franciscan friars in 1493 at 22,000. In that same year, Franciscan friars accompanied Christopher Columbus on his second expedition to the Americas. Franciscan priests said the first Mass in the New World at Port Conception on Hispaniola.

In 1523 and 1524, Franciscan expeditions set out to Mexico from Santo Domingo, a Franciscan base. Then, in 1527, a diocese was formed under the rule of Bishop Juan de Zumárraga, a Franciscan. Zumárraga set up the first printing press in the New World. Moreover, he was the bishop of Mexico City in 1531 when St. Juan Diego Cuauhtlatoatzin, better known as Juan Diego, received his vision of Our Lady of Guadalupe, who has since become the patroness of the Americas.

Some friars, in particular Pedro de Betanzos and Francisco de la Parra, became fluent in the Mayan language. In fact, it is partially thanks to these two Franciscans that experts are able to read Mayan hieroglyphs today. By the end of the sixteenth century, churches dotted Mexico and the Franciscans had spread their missionary activity to North and South America.

In 1573, the Franciscans arrived in Florida. By 1675 there were as many as 40 friars overseeing as many as 36 missions in Florida. This, however, was the apex of Franciscan missionary activity in Florida since the conflict between England and Spain over that portion of the New World was heating up. By 1706 the majority of Franciscan missions in Florida were inoperative.

While Texas remained connected to New Spain, Franciscan missionaries spread throughout the area. Some missionaries went so far as to call the vast area occupied by Texas, New Mexico, Arizona, and California "The New Kingdom of St. Francis." In the eighteenth century, 21 missions were established in Texas, operated by more than 160 friars. Thousands of American Indians were baptized during this time.

The Franciscans began their missionary activity in California in 1769. Bl. Junípero Serra founded 21 missions from San Diego to San Francisco. The Franciscan missionary activity in this region led to an estimated 80,000 baptisms over the next century. The work of Junípero Serra was instrumental in the settlement of California.

The Franciscans were also active in the English American colonies. They assisted the Jesuits in Maryland, New York, Pennsylvania, Kentucky, Michigan, Illinois, and Minnesota between 1672 and 1699.

Many of the Franciscan missionaries gave up their lives for the faith. These martyrs are remembered for their bravery and their fidelity to the mission to spread the Gospel of Christ to the ends of the earth, even at the cost of their own lives. Indeed, without the bravery of such men, America would not be the place it is today.

Franciscan provinces in Europe sent Franciscans over to the United States in the early 1800s. Fr. Michael Egan, O.F.M., an Irish Franciscan, accepted an invitation from Catholics at Lancaster, Pennsylvania, to administer to their spiritual needs. Arriving in 1802, he eventually became the first bishop of Philadelphia in 1808 after Rome received a positive review of Fr. Egan by Archbishop John Carroll. The Diocese of Philadelphia at the time included Pennsylvania, Delaware, and parts of New Jersey. Bishop Egan died in 1814.

In the late 1800s, the Franciscans took charge of parishes and schools throughout the United States. The number of Franciscans steadily grew until the 1960s, when it experienced a decline. American Franciscans typically work in friaries, missions, and schools. Some are academic while others are not. The Franciscans in the United States are dedicated to the poor and the suffering. This is especially true of the Franciscan Friars of the Immaculate, founded in the 1970s, which operates in New York and elsewhere.

In the Americas today, the Franciscans carry with them the example of their spiritual father, St. Francis of Assisi, and strive to emulate his life of penance, dedicated poverty, and commitment to helping the poor. They seek to be a light to others through their holiness and their particular apostolates. The Franciscan impact on the New World was far-reaching and continues to produce positive results among the people of North and South America. The vision of St. Francis and his particular way of following Christ have inspired tens of thousands of Franciscans over the last five centuries since Columbus, a Franciscan tertiary, discovered the Americas. Many cities in the United States—Los Angeles, San Diego, San Francisco, San Antonio—are named after local Franciscan missions. The Franciscans extended the reign of Christ geographically, baptized thousands of people, and helped to settle the New World through their missionary zeal. The life of St. Francis continues to have a profound impact on countless people today, in the Americas and elsewhere.

The Election of Pope Francis

On February 28, 2013, Pope Benedict XVI announced his resignation as pope. This resignation was the first time a pope had stepped down since Pope Gregory XII reluctantly gave up the papacy in 1415 to end the Western Schism. It was also the first time a pope had willingly resigned since Pope Celestine V in 1294. This completely unexpected move meant that a papal election was inevitable. The conclave met on March 12, 2013, to decide who the next pope would be. The next day, the cardinals elected Jorge Mario Bergoglio, the Archbishop of Buenos Aires, Argentina, who took the name Francis.

The election of Francis was special for many reasons. He is the first Jesuit pope, the first pope from the Southern Hemisphere, the first pope from the Americas, and the first non-European pope since Pope Gregory III in 741. He was also the first pope to take the name of Francis.

The relationship between Francis of Assisi and the popes of his era is apropos of Pope Francis taking up his name. Francis of Assisi received the call to rebuild Christ's church, which was in shambles. Initially, Francis believed that Jesus was talking about the church at San Damiano; later on, he realized that the Lord was referring to the entire Catholic Church. Eventually, Francis made his way to Rome to seek papal approval of his way of life. It is said that Pope Innocent III had a dream that Francis was holding up the papal basilica and that this dream inspired him to accept the rule of Francis's way of life. These facts indicate that Pope Francis, too, intends to be a reformer who seeks to bring about greater simplicity in the church and to stir up the Church's zeal for the poor.

When Francis stepped out on the balcony, he gave an eminently simple impression. Shortly after being elected pope, instead of approaching the people on the steps of a pedestal on the balcony in St. Peter's square, Pope Francis chose to stand on the same level as the cardinals around him. Furthermore, he refused to wear the traditional mozzetta that is usually worn by popes upon their election and instead chose to wear a simple white cassock, with his own pectoral cross rather than a fancier one made of gold. He also decided to have his fisherman's ring made out of silver, not gold. Pope Francis then humbly asked the people gathered in St. Peter's Square to pray over him.

When he received the congratulations of the cardinals, Francis did not sit on the papal throne but accepted their congratulations standing up. Finally, when the evening was over, Francis decided to take the bus back to his hotel instead of riding in the papal vehicle. He decided not to live in the papal residence, either, but to reside in the Vatican guest house instead.

Pope Francis explained that he chose the name Francis because Cardinal Cláudio Hummes from Brazil had told him, when it was clear that he would be elected pope during the conclave, not to forget the poor. This made him think of St. Francis. Pope Francis has expressed great admiration for the saint, saying of him that he "brought to Christianity an idea of poverty against the luxury, pride, vanity of the civil and ecclesiastical powers of the time. He changed history."

The pope's decision to call himself Francis demonstrated creativity, for this was the first time since Pope Lando in 913-914 that a pope had not called himself by the name of one of his predecessors. Even then, Lando was that pope's birth name. One would have to go back to Pope Romanus in 897 to find a pope with an original name that may have been different from his birth name.

The coat of arms of Pope Francis does not explicitly convey his connection to Francis. It is rather simple, comprising the Jesuit symbol, HIS, on a blue field, surrounded by three other prominent symbols: a sun, an eight-pointed star, and a cluster of spikenard. IHS is a monogram of Jesus since it is a reflection of the first three letters of Jesus' name in Greek (i.e., iota, eta, and sigma). The star is a symbol of Our Lady, and the spikenard is a symbol of St. Joseph. For this reason, it could be said that Pope Francis has the symbols of the Holy Family on his coat of arms.

While there are no explicitly Franciscan symbols in Pope Francis's coat of arms, it is possible to derive an implicit connection to St. Francis of Assisi if one uses his or her imagination. The Jesuit symbol of the IHS monogram, inside the sun and the three nails, can be seen as relating to St. Francis of Assisi. The three nails represent the nails that pierced Christ's hands and feet. Francis's stigmata reflected these very wounds of Christ. In fact, his earliest biographers, including Thomas of Celano and St. Bonaventure, claim that there were nails in Francis's hands and feet. As for the sun, recall that toward the end of his life, St. Francis wrote his "Canticle to Brother Sun," the first creature for which he thanks God in the canticle. While it is improbable that the Ignatian symbol was intended to demonstrate this symbolism, there remains an unintentional, implicit connection.

The election of Pope Francis has already had profound effects, even though scarcely over one year has passed since he became pope. The faith of Catholics is reinvigorated; unbelievers are pleasantly surprised; and the media can't seem to get enough of the charismatic pontiff. While the pope is charismatic, it is easy to recognize that he possesses not only a magnetic personality but also, more importantly, the Holy Spirit. May the Lord bless Pope Francis and help him to lead the Catholic Church wisely. The next chapter will explore in detail Pope Francis's Franciscan spirituality.

The Franciscan Spirituality of the Pope

Pope Francis is, of course, a Jesuit. For this reason alone, Pope Francis's spirituality cannot be entirely defined by the Franciscan charism. At the same time, much can be said about Francis's Franciscan spirituality. His attraction to St. Francis is evident since, after all, he chose to be called after this saint from Assisi; but what is it about the pope's spirituality that is explicitly Franciscan? The pope's Franciscan spirituality rests on three important points: (1) his concern for the poor, (2) his concern for simplicity, and (3) his concern for nature, in the form of environmental advocacy.

Like his namesake, Francis has a deep love of the poor. We have to remember that it was his fellow cardinal's advice to remember the poor that inspired Bergoglio to choose the name Francis. A few days after he was elected pope, Francis declared that he wanted a church for the poor. He wants the whole of humanity to be concerned about the well-being of the poor and to cooperate together so as to care for the needs of those who are suffering the most. This solicitude for the poor is demonstrated by Bergoglio's actions. He celebrated Holy Thursday Mass at a juvenile detention center and washed the feet of youths, including women, something that had never been done before by a pope. He is also touched by the plight of the poor and is said to sneak out at night, dressed in ordinary clerical garments, so as to distribute food to those in need. And what is the reason for Pope Francis's actions? As he expressed it, those who serve the poor serve Christ. Of course, this is an echo of what Jesus himself said in Matthew 25:31-46, in the parable of the sheep and the goats.

Francis's love for poverty and his solicitude for the poor is something that Pope Francis yearns for the Catholic Church to emulate. The pope teaches that, for us to be able to help the poor, we must live simply and cultivate an attitude that is open to sharing. He was not pleased with bishops who spent lavish amounts on their own comforts, and he publicly reproached the so-called "bishop of bling" in Germany. Furthermore, he is often drawn to the poorest people in his midst, comforting his flock with his kisses, embraces, prayers, and reassurances. He is a good shepherd who models himself after the Good Shepherd. He is solicitous for his flock, and he desires the faithful to follow in his footsteps.

Like John Paul II and Benedict XVI, Pope Francis is an advocate for the environment. Recall that St. John Paul II declared St. Francis of Assisi the patron saint of ecology in 1979. Care for creation was an issue that always remained close to the heart of John Paul II. The same can be said of Pope

Benedict XVI, who declared in *Caritas in Veritate* that human beings must respect creation and learn how to foster virtues that will enable us to live in harmony with our brothers and sisters and with all of God's creatures.

One way to recognize the importance of St. Francis for Pope Francis is the significance of the poor man from Assisi for St. Ignatius of Loyola, the founder of the Society of Jesus, which is the religious order of which Pope Francis is a member. Before his conversion, Ignatius was like Francis in many ways, attracted to battle and the goods of the world, including money, women, and parties. When a cannonball struck him in the knee, however, he was confined to a bed, where he began to read the lives of the saints. The life of St. Francis of Assisi struck Ignatius deeply, and he felt compelled to imitate him rather than to advance in the world. Through the impact of St. Francis, St. Ignatius of Loyola reformed his life and became the founder of the Society of Jesus. Today we have a Jesuit pope, who knows how important Francis was for Ignatius— and how important he is for the world—which is why he chose to be named after Francis of Assisi.

The examples of St. Francis of Assisi and of Pope Francis signify an important message to our society: the purpose of our existence is defined not by our possessions but by our relationships with God and with our brothers and sisters. For this reason, of course, detachment from material things is crucial to the Christian life. Without detachment, people tend to close in on themselves and confine their circle of concern to themselves or a limited number of family members. Simplicity and detachment enable Christians to combat the vices of selfishness and pride, and prepare them for service to the poor, thus enabling them to follow the teachings of Jesus more closely. May the example of Pope Francis inspire Christians everywhere to live simple lives, respect the earth, and come to the assistance of the poor.

The Importance of St. Francis for Our Time

St. Francis of Assisi is a tremendously important saint for our time. His emphasis on humility, poverty, and concern for the poor are perennial calls in keeping with the core message of Jesus; they are biblically based, radical, and prophetic. No Christian can argue against the importance the Gospels laid on being humble—that is, poor in spirit—or against Jesus' teaching that his followers were to feed the hungry, give drink to the thirsty, and clothe the naked. This call, because it stands against the spirit of the world, is also radical and prophetic. It is a calling for each Christian to repent and for Christians everywhere to become countercultural by rejecting the materialistic ideologies that media organizations and advertising agencies inject into Western society's consciousness.

Our capitalistic society emphasizes pulling oneself up by one's own bootstraps and making one's own way to the top of the economic ladder, or as high as one can possibly reach. While there is nothing inherently wrong with making a legitimate and honest living, the emphasis on individuality that pervades our society often causes people to overlook the plight of the poor or even to believe that the poor owe their impoverished state to their own purported laziness. While this may be true of some of the poor, it is not fair to make sweeping judgments that allege all of the poor to be slothful parasites who live off taxpayers' hard-earned money.

In addition to this widespread bias against the poor, our society is thoroughly materialistic. Consumerism promises happiness, as if the acquisition of novel technologies, exciting vehicles, and spacious homes were capable of satisfying all the wants of the human heart. Many people today have traded out church attendance on Sundays for shopping in malls. Name brands become patron saints, and vendors become idolized; greed is sated, and mammon is worshipped, while the poor are left to starve and die in the streets.

The joy St. Francis derived from his poverty clearly demonstrates that the spirit and promises of consumerism are but lies craftily formulated by the devil. True happiness comes from the knowledge that one is loved by God and is being faithful to the Lord of heaven and earth, to whom belong all good things. True happiness comes about through spiritual communion with family members and friends and through a clean conscience and service to the poor. True happiness comes about through detachment from material goods and attachment to God. Our society's tendency to waste is tied to consumerism. The Western world wastes a large amount of food, water, time, money, and energy that could be used to alleviate the suffering of the poor.

Francis's love of nature and his status as the patron saint of ecology shine a light on our society's lack of concern to God's creation. Today, when nature is seen as raw material to be exploited at will without regard for its future preservation or the effects its use may have on other people, it is more important than ever to bring back to life Francis's vision of a cosmos that has sprung forth from God and is bound together precisely because of this divine origin. Recognition of this dependence on divine providence is necessary if human beings are to realize that they are not the rulers of creation but merely its stewards, who have a responsibility to use nature in accordance with the laws of God. For this reason, human beings are called to discover the laws of ecological equilibrium and ought to be careful not to disrupt sensitive ecosystems. At the same time, an overemphasis on nature over and against human beings would be wrong. This is where Francis's solicitude for the poor comes into play. The poor must be given a home and must be permitted to use the resources to which they have a right.

Perhaps the most important reason why St. Francis is significant for our time is because his devotion to Jesus Christ and his call to Christians to get back to basics—by living lives of penance in accordance with the Gospel—are so fitting for our society. This spirit of Christianity is sadly missing from many Christians' lives, and the result is scandal. Francis, by contrast, was an image of Jesus Christ crucified, who in turn is the perfect image of God the Father. By following in the footsteps of St. Francis of Assisi, Christians will be better able to imitate the life of Christ and will be strengthened to take up a life dedicated to penance, prayer, and service. The world needs the spirit of Jesus; it needs the Holy Spirit; it needs the Gospel. Only by being faithful to our baptismal promises will we transform the world from within and thereby prepare God's creation for the renewal of the earth. May St. Francis inspire Christians everywhere to follow the Gospel more closely. St. Francis of Assisi, pray for us!

References and Suggestions for Further Reading

Armstrong, Regis J. and Ignatius C. Brady, trans. *Francis and Clare: The Complete Works*. The Classics of Western Spirituality. New York/Mahwah, NJ: Paulist, 1982.

———. *True Joy: The Wisdom of Francis and Clare.* Edited by Doug Fisher. New York/Mahwah, NJ: Paulist, 1996.

Bergoglio, Jose Mario and Abraham Skorka. *On Heaven and Earth.* Translated by Alejandro Bermudez and Howard Goodman. Edited by in Spanish by Diego F. Rosemberg. New York: Image, 2010.

Bodo, Murray. *The Threefold Way of Saint Francis.* New York/Mahwah, NJ: Paulist, 2000.

Bonaventure. *The Life of St. Francis of Assisi: A Biography of Saint Francis of Assisi and Stories of His Followers.* Charlotte, NC: TAN, 2010.

———. *The Soul's Journey into God; The Tree of Life; The Life of St. Francis.* Translated by Ewert Cousins. The Classics of Western Spirituality. New York: Paulist, 1978.

Burr, David. *The Spiritual Franciscans: From Protest to Persecution in the Century After Saint Francis.*

University Park: The Pennsylvania State University
Press, 2001.

Chesterton, G. K. *Saint Francis of Assisi*. Peabody, MA:
Hendrickson, 2008.

Clare of Assisi. *The Lady: Clare of Assisi: Early Documents*.
Edited and translated by Regis J. Armstrong. New York:
New City Press, 2006.

Cook, William R. *Francis of Assisi: The Way of Poverty and
Humility*. Eugene, OR: Wipf & Stock, 1989.

Cowley, Patrick. *Franciscan Rise and Fall*. London: J. M. Dent &
Sons, 1933.

Cunningham, Lawrence S. *Francis of Assisi: Performing the
Gospel*. Grand Rapids, MI: William B. Eerdmans, 2004.

"Franciscans in the Americas." *Epic World History: Expanding
the world into first global age.*
http://epicworldhistory.blogspot.com/2012/06/franci
scans-in-americas.html. Accessed June 9, 2014.

House, Adrian. *Francis of Assisi: A Revolutionary Life*. Mahwah,
NJ: Hidden Spring, 2001.

Martin, Valerie. *Salvation: Scenes from the Life of St. Francis.* New York: Alfred A. Knopf, 2001.

Simsic, Wayne. *Living the Wisdom of St. Francis.* New York/Mahwah, NJ: Paulist, 2001.

Talbot, John Michael and Steve Rabey. *The Lessons of St. Francis: How to Bring Simplicity and Spirituality into Your Daily Life.* New York: Plume, 1997.

Talbot, John Michael. *Reflections on St. Francis.* Collegeville, MN: Liturgical Press, 2009.

Thomas of Celano. *The Francis Trilogy of Thomas of Celano: The Life of Saint Francis; The Remembrance of the Desire of Soul; The Treatise on the Miracles of Saint Francis.* Edited by Regis J. Armstrong, J. A. Wayne Hellmann, William J. Short. Hyde Park, NY: New City Press, 2004.

Thompson, Augustine. *Francis of Assisi: A New Biography.* Ithaca, NY: Cornell University Press, 2012.

Please enjoy the first two chapters of The Life and Times of Jesus (Part 1), written by Michael J. Ruszala, as available from Wyatt North Publishing.

Introduction

By worldly terms, Jesus of Nazareth was born to an insignificant family, raised in an insignificant town; he was a lowly subject in an insignificant province of an empire ruled by cruel men over 1,400 miles across the sea. And yet Jesus of Nazareth did more to change the course of world history than has any other historical figure. Even his enemies did not deny his otherworldly power, and his followers would call him 'Lord' over Lord-Caesar. Though his own kingdom was "not of this world," his own once-persecuted and -outlawed followers would overcome the pagan Roman Empire within three centuries, paving the way for an almost thoroughly Christianized Europe for millennia to come. Even today, over 2.1 billion people across every region and continent call themselves Christians, such that nearly one in three persons in the world today consider themselves followers of Christ. And while today's secularized and globalized society has tried to declare its independence from the preacher of Nazareth, it cannot help that it owes much of its own sense of justice, morality, peace, and tolerance to Jesus and his followers. Although many today, looking back at the course of world and European history, assume that society has moved beyond the Way of Christ, G. K. Chesterton reminds us that "Christianity has not been tried and found wanting; it has been found difficult and not tried."

The man called the 'Word' of God by John the Evangelist (in Jn. 1:1) is not known to have ever stained a papyrus with any lines for posterity, yet the books that deal with the implications of what he said and did fill entire libraries. No book has sold more copies or been more widely translated than the Christian Bible, the heart of which is the Gospels of Christ and all of which, Christians believe, is centered on him even in hidden ways. New alphabets have been invented to record his words; countless monks spent their lives writing them and meditating on them; the printing press was invented to distribute them; missionaries have died trying to spread them; nations were founded to live them freely; charities and hospitals were developed to express them more fully. Workmen curse by his name almost without thinking, so ingrained in the western psyche is the all-pervading legacy of that one solitary life lived two thousand years ago.

While today his words are transmitted by satellite, television, social media, books, CDs, and videos, Jesus' contemporaries heard about him first by word of mouth. They heard wondrous things, and troubling things. They were confronted head-on with the identity of this itinerant preacher as the gossip spread through the marketplace, by the well-side, among workers in the field, and from neighbor to neighbor.

They had to take a side, and that side brought consequences – as did Jesus' acceptance of certain followers from amongst them.

Zacchaeus was one such man. He was a contrarian of sorts, shrewd enough to find an opportunity to make a handsome living for himself off his nation's unfortunate political situation. His career had led him to become the head tax-collector for the Roman occupiers at Jericho, a city known at the time for its lucrative trade of balsam wood. He collected steep tariffs for the Empire and extorted more for himself on items moving through the city, known even today as the oldest city in the world. Tax collecting was a very profitable business but made him few friends really worth having and left his conscience sick. While his wealth kept accumulating, emotionally, the "wee little man" had hit a low point.

As Zacchaeus glumly went along his way one day, he was caught in a first-century traffic jam because the inhabitants of the city – including many people whom Zacchaeus had tricked and pressured – flooded the streets to see and hear for themselves this Jesus, who had by then made quite a stir touring Galilee to the north and visiting Jerusalem to the west. Perhaps Zacchaeus had heard that Jesus had dared to throw out the moneychangers in the Temple for extortion – a very similar business to his own yet far more socially tolerated. Perhaps he had heard about Jesus' miracles, which he believed could only come from God. Perhaps he had heard that one of this rabbi's key disciples – Matthew – had been a notorious tax collector in Capernaum in Galilee before hitting the road with Jesus. Perhaps his conscience was pricked. Zacchaeus didn't know exactly who this man was, but he knew he wanted to see for himself. So he found a way around the push and shove of the crowd. He climbed up into a sycamore fig tree and balanced himself on a branch, unperturbed about what people might think of him. Of course, he never did care about that anyway.

To his surprise, the prophet took note of him. "Zacchaeus, come down quickly, for today I must stay at your house" (Lk. 19:5). Zacchaeus was overjoyed that this holy man noticed him, but the crowds were not at all pleased with Jesus' plan to dine with the chief of the local tax collectors. Of all people in town for Jesus to find! But Zacchaeus' heart was changed that day. He even promised to give alms generously as well as to make full restitution even by the strict standards of Jewish religious law: "Behold, half of my possessions, Lord, I shall give to the poor, and if I have extorted anything from anyone I shall repay it four times over." The Bible doesn't tell us what became of Zaccheaus, but we can imagine that from that day, business was never again as usual for Zaccheaus; and his relationships with the Romans, with the tax collectors, with the townspeople, and with his own carefully procured wealth were forever altered. There were consequences for his choice, and he could never look back. Yet he found something more valuable than all the silver, gold, and trade-portions that he had so shrewdly been collecting.

In the same way, we too are confronted by the person of Jesus. Many people know about Jesus, yet few truly know him. The common people of Judea, Galilee, Samaria, and the regions neighboring greater Palestine knew him in a way that we never can. In some ways we have an advantage over them because of the two-thousand-year tradition of the Church. For many of them, their perspective of him was raw and mostly un-reflected. Jesus asked his disciples what the people thought of him, as to his identity. They replied, "Some say John the Baptist, others Elijah, still others Jeremiah or one of the prophets" (Mt. 16:14). While people still have many false opinions about Jesus, no one would say those things today. But because of the tradition of the Church, we long for what these people had – yet did not know that they had. While many of those people did not understand him, for others the experience of Jesus of Nazareth was sufficient cause to endure social persecution, time in prison, torture, and execution. This book aims to give us a historical glimpse into the first-century experience of Jesus of Nazareth. It will treat in basic terms the religious, political, and cultural situation that set the stage for what St. Paul calls the "fullness of time" (Gal. 4:4). It wasn't a glamorous time. It was more the kind of time that most of us are grateful we don't have to endure. But this book will prepare us to take our place within the crowd, to hear Jesus preach and see him perform mighty deeds, when we open up the Gospels for ourselves. While no one today would say that Jesus is John the Baptist, Elijah, or Jeremiah, we will see for ourselves if we agree with our own contemporaries that Jesus of Nazareth was simply a great man, a noble teacher, a religious founder, and an unfortunate martyr. Or perhaps we agree with the sour-faced scholars who tell us that Jesus of Nazareth was a failed messiah who never intended to found a religion and that the religion bearing his name has done little to further the material progress of the world.

Pope Benedict XVI reflects in *Jesus of Nazareth*, "What did Jesus actually bring, if not world peace, universal prosperity, and a better world? What has he brought? The answer is very simple: God. He has brought God. He has brought the God who formerly unveiled his countenance gradually, first to Abraham, then to Moses and the Prophets.... He has brought God, and now we know his face, now we can call upon him. Now we know the path that we human beings have to take in this world. Jesus has brought God and with God the truth about our origin and destiny: faith, hope, and love."

The Story of a People

Open to the beginning of the New Testament and the genealogy of Jesus is what you will find. Most skip over it while others bravely plough their way through it. But much like Matthew, the writer of the first Gospel, I too feel the need to express before anything else that the story of Jesus does not begin with Jesus of Nazareth. A great history is presupposed – a history that his fellow countrymen would have known as well as we know the names of our own grandparents. The only question is: how far back should we go? For Matthew, the answer was to go back to Abraham, the ancient father of the Jewish people, whom God had called out of the city of Ur in Mesopotamia in a journey of faith to the land of Canaan, later called Palestine. For Luke the Evangelist, the answer was Adam, the father of the human race, emphasizing that Jesus came for all peoples.

Very basically, the history presupposed is that of God's intervention in human affairs, particularly those of the Chosen People, the Children of Israel. The Bible tells us that God spoke to Abraham, bringing him into a covenant with God alone as God, as opposed to the many false gods of his ancestors. As God promised, he made Abraham into a vast people, and that people was later liberated from slavery in Egypt by Moses. The Bible tells us that God spoke to Moses and made a covenant with Moses. And through Moses, God made the people a nation, replete with laws to govern them. Then there was David, the greatest king of Israel, a man "after God's own heart." And the Bible tells us that God spoke to David and made a covenant with him, promising that his kingdom would last forever and even that his son would be God's son. But no sooner had David died than the kingdom was severed in two by a rivalry, never to rise again to the full glory it had known under David. The history of the kings of Israel and Judah became a history of turning away from God and of God punishing the kingdoms for their sins. First the Northern Kingdom was conquered, and the survivors were carried off by the Assyrians in the eighth century BC under King Sennacherib. Then, in the sixth century BC, the Kingdom of Judah to the south was conquered by the Babylonians under King Nebuchadnezzar; and the survivors were marched off to Babylon in chains. Then came Jesus, whom the Bible calls the "Word" of God made flesh (Jn. 1) – Jesus, who told Pilate before his execution, "my kingdom is not of this world." But before Jesus, there came the Persians, then the Greeks, and then the Romans. In 538 BC, the Persians under King Cyrus conquered the Babylonians and allowed the Hebrew captives to return to their homeland and rebuild their Temple in Jerusalem, which King Solomon, the son of David, had first constructed. The Persians held control of Palestine for centuries, but the Jews were fairly content to have the Persians for their rulers since they were better than the alternatives. Then, in 332 BC, Alexander the Great took control of Palestine from the Persians. His reign was vast but short lived. Having died at the age of 33, his empire was given to his heirs and divided into four kingdoms. The Seleucid kingdom to the north and the Ptolemaic kingdom, based in Egypt to the south, would vie between themselves for control of Palestine. Judas Maccabaeus and his brothers led a bloody revolt in the mid-second century BC against Palestine's Seleucid rulers, who were trying to force the Jews to violate Jewish religious laws and customs. Remarkably, the Maccabees did gain independence. Ultimately the Jews assented to become a client kingdom under the Seleucids, granted that they could practice their religion in peace and manage their own affairs. Springing from Jonathan, the brother of Judas Maccabeus, the Jewish Hasmonean dynasty ruled over this semi-independent kingdom in Palestine from 160 to 63 BC.

During the revolt, the Maccabees had made an alliance with the Roman Republic. But as the Republic morphed into the greatest empire the western world has ever known, Palestine, too, fell prey to its ambitions. Pompey conquered Jerusalem in

63 BC, establishing the Roman province of Judea, and killed some 12,000 Jews and desecrated the Temple. When it came to the actual practice of the Jewish religion, however, Pompey learned from his Greek predecessors not to interfere too much – a precedent that would last for the remaining centuries of Roman rule. But the Romans had plenty of areas other than religion in which to impose their power through fear and cruelty. Burdensome taxes were levied to pay for the expanding Roman Empire. The commentator Vermont Royster wrote of the Romans, "There was enslavement of men whose tribes came not from Rome…. And most of all, there was contempt for human life. What, to the strong, was one man more or less in a crowded world?" The slaughter by Pompey was nothing compared to the Roman response to the revolt in Judea, culminating in AD 70, in which around one million Jews lost their lives. Anyone fleeing Jerusalem during the siege was crucified – hundreds every day, such that the first-century Judeo-Roman historian Flavius Josephus recounts that there were not enough crosses for the bodies.

Crucifixion was not invented by the Romans, but it was elaborated sadistically by them. Crucifixion had been used by the Seleucids in Palestine before the Romans, and was used by other powers in the ancient world. The Romans used it as an extreme deterrent and sign of contempt for conquered peoples and for slaves. In fact, the ancient writer Valerius Maximus called it the 'slave's punishment.' Crucifixion was not mentioned in polite Roman society, but soldiers experimented with various forms as a kind of cruel sport. This long and drawn-out form of execution was deplorably common for non-citizens and slaves, and gibbets for crucifixion were placed outside of major cities such as Jerusalem. It struck shame and dread into the hearts of all, lest anyone dare defy the powers that be. Bloody crucifixes were a common sight in the days of Christ, though the Romans did not hesitate to use their many other dreadful ways of punishing or executing insubordinate provincials as well. But not only did the Jews have the Romans to deal with, they were also under the iron hand of Herod the Great, who called himself the 'King of the Jews.'

46727765R00079

Made in the USA
Lexington, KY
13 November 2015